The
Grieving

How the Arts and Art-Marking
Help Us Grieve and Live Our Best Lives

Sheila K. Collins, PhD

Award Winning Author
of *Warrior Mother* and *Stillpoint*

This publication is designed to provide accurate and authoritative information in regard to the subject matter covered. It is sold with the understanding that neither the author nor the publisher is engaged in rendering medical, psychological, or other professional services.

Library of Congress Cataloging-in-Publication Data
Library of Congress Control Number: 2024904500

Names: Collins, Sheila K. author
Title: **The Art of Grieving:** *How Art and Artmaking Help Us Grieve and Live Our Best Lives/*

Sheila K Collins, PhD.
Description: First Edition. /Includes bibliographical references and index / Pittsburgh, PA: Earth Springs Press 2024 /
Identifiers: ISBN **9781732370487** (pbk) ISBN **9781732370494** (ebook)

Subjects: LCSH: Grief. / Bereavement. / Arts—Psychological aspects. / Resilience— (Personality trait)

Classification: Biography and autobiography / Personal Memoirs. / Motivational / Family and Relationships / death grief, bereavement /

Printed in the United States of America on acid-free paper.
Book and cover designed by Christa Varley

7.19.2024

Susan,

Thank you for your
support of grief as a
gift and of using the
arts to experience it.

Sheila K Collins

*On behalf of all who
endure the pain of loss,
and companion others
on this journey that defines
the human condition.*

*May you experience
through the arts,
the spiral path of growth
and insight and savor,
in community rituals,
the gifts that grief so
eloquently bestows.*

Advanced Praise for The Art of Grieving

"The Art of Grieving is both uplifting and educational, shedding light on a subject often marginalized to the detriment of all. Collectively each chapter is relevant for anyone grappling with the inevitability of grief while individually, each chapter explores specific facets of the experience, offering pathways to repurpose the process through artistic endeavors. I highly recommend this unique and long awaited. book."

-Gail Neustadt
Speech Language Pathologist,
Environmental Activist and Author

"Sheila K. Collins, in The Art of Grieving, reveals through her own incredible life experiences, a courage and creativity that has helped her survive and even thrive with dignity, some of life's most grievous losses. Her book shows us how to do the same. Her engaging writing style will have you not wanting to put the book down. You'll want to keep cheering her on, and in doing so, you'll find you're cheering yourself on as you discover new possibilities for engaging with life in creative ways. A must read!"

-Glenda Taylor
Director of the Fellowship of Comparative Religions

The Art of Grieving is a priceless gift to the human family. Dr. Collins' articulation of grief as a spiral is a revolutionary concept that she and I both recognized independently and a major step forward from stage theories of grief. Reading her book is like having a series of enlightening and comforting conversations with a wise, knowledgeable, and experienced companion. I highly recommend and wholeheartedly endorse her book for anyone who has ever experienced loss of any kind and for those who may experience loss in the future. In a word, I recommend it for everyone.

-Grace Terry, MSW
Grief Coach, author of **The Spiral Pathway of Grief**

We need to get good at grieving according to author Sheila K Collins since, as humans we can count on experiencing both big and small losses throughout our lives. The Art of Grieving shows us how to use the arts to grieve well. Partly a beautiful memoir, the book teaches through storied examples and researched materials, the positive neurological impact of art and artmaking on our grieving brains. Each chapter includes a set of activities for the reader's experiential understanding of what the author calls "metabolizing our grief." The readable weaving of personal reflections of a clear, inspiring, writer kept me unable to stop reading. This reminded me of not wanting to leave my husband Jim's side in those last days. They were like this book, so full of exquisite grace.

-Pamela Meadowcroft
Psychologist, founding member of the
Wing and a Prayer Pittsburgh Players

Sheila K Collins offers a profound exploration of how to navigate the complex terrain of grief with grace and purpose. "The Art of Grieving: How the Arts and Art-Making Help Us Grieve and Live Our Best Lives, reflects the author's deep wisdom as an artist and embodied coach. She illuminates a path toward healing and living a more meaningful life even in the face of profound loss. This book beautifully demonstrates the transformative power of art in the grieving process, offering practical tools and resources deeply rooted in the embodied experience. The book's compassionate voice and insightful guidance nurture the reader, providing solace and inspiration on the journey toward healing and wholeness.

-Christine Gautreaux, MSW
Women Connected in Wisdom Co-founder.

I highly recommend The Art of Grieving: How the Arts and Artmaking Help Us Grieve and Live Our Best Lives. Get it. Read it. I promise it will help you and those you love navigate grief every day of your lives. Sheila writes from the soul of a dancer, social worker, and grief advocate profoundly intimate with death, dying, and loss. I, too, travel a somatic path, and agree that Grieving is an Art! It's vital to honor its starring role in the dance of life. Sheila keys us into ways grief can "work its magic when we use the arts to help process our lives." I'm sending The Art of Grieving to my family and friends. I want it in the curriculum of every future leader.

-Cynthia Winton-Henry
Cofounder of InterPlay, author of
The Art of Ensoulment: How to Create From Body and Soul.

"Collins has given us a wise, well-researched guide to grieving's winding path, revealing how communal art-making provides catharsis and connection when loss inevitably strikes. This book is a gift."

-Daniel H. Pink
#1 New York Times bestselling author of THE POWER OF REGRET

In The Art of Grieving, Sheila K. Collins shares compelling personal and professional stories of how engaging in artistic activities such as music, poetry, dance, storytelling, and visual arts can help us process grief. With deep compassion, Collins helps us understand how -- through creative expression and honoring loved ones -- we can heal, enter into a transformative space, and find the courage to embrace life anew after mourning.

-Susan Magsamen, Co-author
with Ivy Ross, Your Brain on Art: How the Arts Transform Us

The Art of Grieving teaches us that grief is about much more than a loved ones' death. Author Sheila K Collins shows us through examples from her own life, and those of her clients, family members, and friends, how to use the arts to process losses of all kinds so that we come to peace, over and over again.

-Rebecca Lindholm
Musician, and InterPlay practitioner

Contents

Foreword

In a world where most of us feel a mounting sense of pain and grief–both individually and collectively–"The Art of Grieving" emerges just in time. This important book serves as a populist treatise on how grieving can become not just a skill, but perhaps the essential skill of our times. It democratizes access to profound insights needed for each of us to navigate the labyrinth of grief with compassion and creativity, singularly and in community.

As founder and executive director of Reimagine, an organization committed to transforming how people from all walks of life engage with loss, adversity, and mortality, I am intimately familiar with grief's tumultuous currents. So, I'm honored to introduce this important work. Sheila seamlessly blends her profound personal journey navigating the rivers of grief with her extensive professional expertise in mental healthcare and, most importantly, her experiences using the arts to process grief. Through intimate and relatable storytelling, she provides a beacon of understanding for readers, inviting us to embark on a journey of healing and curiosity alongside her. By combining her wisdom with practical psychological theory her insights are grounded for everyday application. In doing so, she equips readers with a broader understanding of the myriad ways loss and grief show up in our lives and with the emotional tools to begin using them on our own journeys. In my own professional work with grief and loss, I am guided by a belief that there are only three broad potential responses to grief: 1) Repression: We can attempt to suppress grief's emotional energy. However, we know this is unhealthy, ineffective, and almost impossible to sustain. 2) Harmful externalization: We let it out, but in ways that are unhealthy, leading toward further suffering for ourselves, our loved ones, our communities, and even the planet. 3) Healthy externalization. So, if we can't keep it in, and we need to let it out in ways that are good for us and others, what are those ways?

Western culture's answer to this last question is typically to point us toward therapy or counseling. However, this book illuminates a crucial macro truth hiding in plain sight: there are endless healthy, creative possibilities for how we might process our pain and grief, though these avenues are rarely taught or understood. "The Art of Grieving" illuminates these powerful pathways, walking the reader through a profound exploration of healthy externalization through the arts, and revealing that each of our lives offer boundless creative potential for healing and transformation.

But those words "art" and "creativity" can often feel scary, inaccessible, or overly vulnerable for non-professional artists. Sheila, however, is able to explicate creativity in ways we can all grasp: in fact, she re-labels it "folk art," emphasizing how modes of creative expression can be developed "from, by, or for, just plain folks," making hers a uniquely democratic and empowering approach to healing. Through our own creative expressions— storytelling, music, painting, writing, dancing, or calling on artists to perform these arts on our behalf —Sheila shows how we can externalize our grief in ways that are cathartic and generative, and that work for each of us, no matter who we are. For me personally, music has provided pathways to process loss, and Sheila's examples from Leonard Cohen to Tina Turner to Taylor Swift offer anecdotes for everyone.

I have had the personal privilege of witnessing Sheila's commitment to communal healing firsthand. At Reimagine–we rely on leaders in the community to spark a cultural sea change from the bottom up. Sheila is a uniquely inspiring voice in this community. She has hosted public events and workshops that introduce audiences to various artistic outlets for grief. She has participated in public communal poetry readings and shown up personally in online breakout rooms to care for isolated members of the community in need of a friendly ear. Sheila walks the walk.

At the heart of Sheila's work lies a profound resonance with the mission of Reimagine. She embodies our ethos of facing life's challenges with love and curiosity. As Reimagine embarks on our own new journey to launch an online social platform that facilitates the healthy externalization of pain in community, Sheila's book serves as a North Star for what that could look like in practice. "Dance with everything," Sheila advocates. If everyone were to read this book, internalize her wisdom, and then transform their grief as she describes, I am confident there would be more dancing and more health and healing, both for ourselves and the world.

Brad Wolfe, Founder & Executive Director, Reimagine

Introduction

"How many children do you have?"

    It was the question I dreaded the most—the question that would come up early on, in nearly every conversation I had, when my husband and I moved from Fort Worth, Texas to Pittsburgh, Pennsylvania in 2005. What made this simple "getting to know you" question so difficult was that just nine months prior to these conversations, our forty-two-year-old daughter, Corinne, had died of breast cancer. And then there was the other detail in my biography. Seven years prior to Corinne's death, our son Kenneth died of AIDS after a four-year journey with that disease, just after his thirty-first birthday. When I was able to somehow get through my own discomfort to communicate these facts, not just distract from the question by talking about my other son Kevin and my granddaughter Kyra living in California, the person who asked the question would say, with an embarrassed or shocked look on their face, "Oh, I am so sorry."

    Some people would then back away, create more space between us, and look around the room, searching for a way to exit the space gracefully. If the person was able to stay in the conversation, our next exchanges were attempts by both of us to alleviate the cloud of discomfort rising between us. I would try to recover from the fact that I had not presented the information well and begin reassuring the person that it wasn't all as bad as it sounded. They would tell me some version of how "I could never handle things as well as you seem to be handling them," or, "I could never survive the death of a child, and you have lost two."

And me? I was left feeling isolated. A pariah, someone to be avoided, as though what has happened to me in my life might be contagious.

Loss is common, it's inevitable; we can count on experiencing many episodes of loss in a lifetime, often coming when we least expect them. If we didn't know that before March of 2020 and the big global shut down, we surely know it now. Though by 2022, in an editor's response to an early version of a proposal for this book, I was told that publishers are not interested in anything related to the pandemic. By the time the book would be published, people would be ready to move on.

But it is impossible to fully move on. If we can pause a moment to reflect on lessons learned, as we emerge from the isolation and fear for our lives and our health that the pandemic inflicted on us, we see that death is not all we need to grieve. There are many types of loss that we grieve, many of which the pandemic illuminated. There's the loss of normalcy, of the familiar, of what we expected to be doing in this period and time of our lives. The loss of what we counted on, jobs, paychecks, attending sporting events and theaters, socializing in groups of friends, and being able to travel freely. And let's take a pause to acknowledge some of the people, places, and activities we have loved that are not coming back.

These same types of losses have impacted people differently in relationship to multiple factors, such as availability of resources, timing in our own life cycles, and temperament. Each loss and our grieving of it changes us and our lives in both expected and unexpected ways. Since grieving is the way we process our losses, I have become convinced of its importance. Since losses will continue to happen, grieving is a necessary set of skills—an art we need to get good at to have a satisfying life.

My story of awkward exchanges in meeting new people after the death of my two children is most likely not unfamiliar to you. In the "get over it" swagger that passes for a successful life skill, mourners are often left in social isolation to "fake it 'til we make it," being careful not to disturb other people's attempts to do the same. As I attempted to grieve and process my own losses, I confronted how much I didn't know about grieving, or about supporting others through their grief as I was going through mine. This seemed more than a bit odd, my having had a thirty-year career as a mental health professional. I was not taught, nor were other mental health professionals of my generation taught, the answers to the questions raised by my own life experiences. Even though I'd taught and mentored emerging helping professionals, accompanying hundreds of clients on their journeys through grief and loss, there was still so much I didn't understand about grief and the grieving process, especially our culture's discomfort with it. I began looking for answers to the following questions and will be exploring those answers with you in this book:

- How did we get grief so wrong in our Western culture?
- What does healthy grieving look like?
- What helps and what hinders the grieving process?
- How can we become more comfortable supporting family members, friends and neighbors going through it?
- How should we relate to the sorrows of the world that technology brings into our living rooms and onto our handheld devices most days?
- My own experiences showed me that grief has some gifts, and I wondered: Why didn't I know about them? Shouldn't we all know about them?

As a teacher and therapist accustomed to giving homework assignments to students and clients, I decided to give myself a homework assignment. It began with imagining: "What if we assume, in the art of living a life, that loss is a frequent, episodic occurrence, expected to happen throughout our years, and that grieving needs to be an art we practice and eventually get good at?" Next, I wondered, "Is it possible that many of our societal troubles occur because we don't know how to grieve well?" Perhaps grieving is made more difficult because communal grieving processes are not in place to help individuals and communities grieve losses when they happen, especially losses due to large-scale societal forces. And then, as a dancer and improvisational performer, I wondered, "Could the arts be tools to express our hopes and sorrows while offering ways to memorialize and celebrate those that have gone before us, much like what happened for our ancestors, and still does in many of the world's indigenous cultures?"

Seeds for my appreciation of the arts as a vehicle to help us grieve were planted while I was working on a previous manuscript. I was preparing to travel from Pittsburgh to Iowa City to attend a writing workshop. My husband knew that I was working on a memoir that discussed the events surrounding the deaths of two of our three adult children. Saying goodbye to him, we hugged, and I headed down the stairs to get in the car that was taking me to the airport. From over my shoulder, I heard his message of casual concern, "I hope you find something more pleasant to write about."

I knew my husband did not understand my turning *towards* memories of our family tragedies and writing about them. To him, this seemed a version of picking at one's sores. I knew he wanted to protect me from what he saw as potential self-harm. In the preface to the manuscript that became *Warrior Mother: Fierce Love, Unbearable Loss and Rituals that Heal,* I described how a powerful connection had formed between my art, my writing, and my grieving.

The writer's workshop in Iowa City was held a couple of weeks after the town had suffered a significant flood. I brought home two empty sandbags, like the thousands of bags of sand stacked as barricades against the rising water. My empty sandbags had been decorated and made into handbags by artists in the community, then sold to raise money to help the local Habitat for Humanity fund the cleanup effort. Arriving home, I came into our bedroom and laid down, my decorated sandbags alongside a folder of my writing. "My writings are *my* sandbags," I told Rich. "We have to make art out of what happens to us, or at least something useful, and we don't get to pick what that is."

It was somewhat natural that I would turn to the arts to assist me in metabolizing my experiences of loss. Throughout a long life, for reasons that I often couldn't explain, even to myself, I have continued to identify with my first profession as a dancer and practitioner of improvisation. Dancers know that words and reason, though often helpful, are not sufficient. We need art and the rituals it provides as containers and vehicles for the expression of our emotions and our stories. If done on our behalf, artistic expression—music, theater, poetry—provides access to the framework of our emotions and the distance we need to discover the meaning in our own experiences. When making art, drawing, painting, cooking, gardening, flower arranging, decorating, we are taken into liminal space—that "space between the worlds"—where processing the losses of our lives can take place.

In 1993, according to the World Health Organization, approximately two million people were newly diagnosed with AIDS, raising the total since the start of the AIDS pandemic to more than fifteen million. In the US, most of them were gay men. My son was one of them.

In addition to the fact that there were little-to-no effective treatments for the disease, Ken had been advised by the AIDS Outreach Center that since he wanted to keep his job, he shouldn't tell anyone, even his best friend, about his diagnosis. They had lawyers that would help him get his job back, but the better path was for him and his family to keep his diagnosis a secret. This was the big picture of what our family was dealing with when we came together in the spring of 1994 from Texas, Oregon, and Southern California in a hotel at the airport in San Francisco for an AIDS, Medicine, and Miracles Conference. There were two-hundred or so professional caregivers, physicians, nurses, social workers, alternative medicine practitioners, and patients. Dazed, and in and out of depression and denial, we were hoping for a miracle, and completely shocked to learn that, though the conference had been advertised for families, we were the only family members present.

There were helpful demonstrations and suggestions— acupuncture can alleviate the side effects created by Western medicines; meditation practice offers relief for the anxiety inherent in facing a life-threatening future. But it was the lunch time presentation that stays with me to this day. There we were, in a large gathering space, seated at tables, opening our sandwiches from their plastic wrappings as the lights came up on a performance space elevated slightly above us. The session was not to be a lecture or demonstration, but a presentation, a performance by the Wing It Performance Ensemble, directed by InterPlay founder and improvisational artist Phil Porter. I had recently been introduced to InterPlay through its other founder Cynthia Winton-Henry, a dancing minister, and, at that time, leader in the Sacred Dance Guild. I was amazed at our good fortune in being able to see the company perform.

The theme was AIDS and the group played with words we called out from the audience. They created dances, songs, and stories on the spot and in the moment around themes like fear, taboos, health, being gay, medicine, and, of course, miracles. Later, when I learned more about the InterPlay system, I realized there was a name for what was transpiring. The artists were dancing, singing, and storytelling *on our behalf*. They were doing one of the things the arts do best for mourners: affirming our experience and expressing for us what we need to have expressed in order to process the experiences of our lives.

According to the CDC, each year in the US, 242,100 people are diagnosed with breast cancer, most of them women. In 1990, my best friend Rose was one of them. In 2002, my forty-year-old daughter Corinne was one of them. After several years of treatment, both died of their disease.

But something important happened in the culture between the time of my son's death, Rose's death, and Corinne's diagnosis. Thanks to the Race for the Cure and other fundraising and awareness-raising efforts, pink ribbons were everywhere — on shampoo bottles and Kleenex boxes, on t-shirts and computer memes. My daughter and our family were surrounded and held up by communities of people and their acceptance and support. There was such a stark difference in the way we felt or didn't feel supported through the losses of our son and our daughter. We were so focused on keeping Ken's situation from becoming public knowledge for fear of other people's errant moral judgements that we felt very alone. With Corrine, we felt the uplifting support of the community around us. This difference may also be due to the extent of fear of the two diseases and the expected death rates from each of them, but whatever the reason, having community support made the experience of processing our grief, and traversing the challenging path we were on, less lonely and more easeful to do.

After my memoir was published, to get the book out, I created a version of Interplay's Dancing on Behalf that I called *Performing the Book*. Following the convention of authors reading excerpts from their work, I would read a snippet from the book and then call an InterPlay form familiar to the InterPlay company that had joined me. They would perform stories from their own lives suggested by the reading, on behalf of themselves and the witnesses. For people who attended the book events and performances, one could sense their relief, see their elation, and feel their gratitude for the opportunity to confront the most essential reality of the human condition. In receiving my expression of love, loss, and grief, as well as the expression of my fellow improvisational InterPlay performers, they recognized something of their own stories. At the conclusion of an event, audience members seemed reluctant to leave the gathering space and the discussions they felt encouraged to have with one another.

In contrast to the positive outcomes and responses to the stories and themes of loss and grief in my book, I also received an education on the extent of reluctance and fearful avoidance in our culture for anything having to do with grief, loss, and mourning. I met with other women authors who shared stories about being told, as I was, by people in the publishing world some version of "grief doesn't sell." I remember telling Jack Canfield, "I want to learn how to stop scaring people."

Taking steps towards finding some answers, I began to use my weekly blog, which I had started as a writing practice, to look through the lens of grief at what was happening in my own personal world as well as what the larger world was dealing with. This became a way to hold a conversation, often taboo in our Western culture, as people on my list began to respond and relate to what I wrote.

My own questions about dealing with loss, grief, mourning and bereavement, and questions and inquiries raised by people in online searches of these topics led me to realize we're all somewhat illiterate when it comes to appreciating the importance and value of grieving and about what we need to do to grieve our losses well. It is widely recognized that death is a taboo subject, one that we actively avoid, but I suspect our lack of comfort with and willingness to discuss death is a product of our positivity-addicted culture, of keeping the bad news to ourselves. Ram Dass suggests, "We protect ourselves from suffering—our own and from each other. When you love someone, you don't want to lay your suffering on them or your fears." And maybe more importantly, "you are afraid if you open your heart to further suffering it will overwhelm you." The result, of course, is a lack of connection and mutual support, hunger for a community whose members share their hard-earned wisdom in how to handle life's most enduring challenges.

Topics for my weekly blog, *Dancing with Everything*, included anything we were currently encountering in our Western cultural life, or anything emerging or relevant in my personal life, looking at each topic through the lens of loss and the need to grieve it well. This included the big societal challenges we're facing, like climate change, racial reckoning, living with a spreading life-threatening pandemic, and later emerging from the effects of it, including smaller personal losses, the illness or death of a loved one, the estrangement from a loved one, challenges to one's health or abilities, the loss of a job or career, the death of a pet. The loss of identity seemed to emerge as part of many losses, as well as the loss of the dream of what we had expected or hoped for. My weekly writing practice and its subject have spawned this book and its mission to heal the wounded hearts of our popular Western culture, and of us, its members.

Another way that the arts can help us to grieve is when we are willing to be the art-maker—the practitioner, the writer, the storyteller, the dancer, the painter. Here, witnesses and fellow artists hold and support us, as does the framework of the art itself, to metabolize our experiences, making wisdom available to us in our future lives.

It was thirty years ago, and people who were there remember different aspects of the experience. It was an InterPlay workshop that my husband and I attended at Dorothy's Rest Retreat Center in California, the fall after our son had been diagnosed with AIDS. I can still picture the room, narrow with windows all along one side, their light reflecting in streaks across the wooden floor. We're barefoot as modern dancers usually are. I remember the four "angels" standing at the four corners of the room, guarding the sacred space as we prepared to do a group movement piece. It was a ritual, if you will, around the situation that our family was facing. My husband Richard remembers running in circles around the room. Running just to be running. Randomly running as though he might never stop running.

In a recent conversation, my friend Susan told me something I don't remember doing, but it makes sense that, given the opportunity, I would have done it. Susan, who was a new member of Wing It at the time remembers the piercing sound of my mother wail. Phil remembers playing the part of my son, and me playing the part of the mother who must practice letting go of him. I reminded Phil recently that he had said to me before we began, "When I'm ready to leave, you must let me go," and I agreed to that condition. Phil doesn't remember saying that, but we both agree that sounds like something an adult child would say to their mother.

Later, when we were processing what had happened during the ritual, he admitted that it was a lot harder for him to leave than he had imagined it would be. I agreed that it was harder for me as well to let him go, which seemed a confirmation of how hard we hold onto life and those we love, no matter what happens or what previous agreements we've made. It's also a confirmation of how different it is to imagine doing something and then actually doing it, or even taking an action that represents it.

In this dance, this communal art-making, we faced the reality of our lives and moved in response to it with the support of one another. I can't articulate how this experience changed me, but I know that it did. It changed us all—makers, performers, and witnesses. One of the "angels," a young man in his twenties, like my son, came out to the group with something he had not told anyone: that he himself was dealing with AIDS. Knowing what I now know about grieving, and the need for a community to hold us, I look back with incredible gratitude that the universe, or whoever is in charge of such things, provided this opportunity for me. And I see now why I became so dedicated to making opportunities for others to use the arts and art-making to process their own grief, as well as the grief inflicted on all of us from the large political and social systems in which we are entangled.

An important gift to my understanding of how the arts help us to grieve and process our lives came with the 2023 release of Susan Magsamen and Ivy Ross's book *Your Brain on Art: How the Arts Transform Us*. As non-invasive brain imaging has become available to researchers, it is now possible for scientists to understand why and how people respond to the arts. I celebrate the launch of this virtual feast of scientific evidence and the compelling stories that support the message of this book—the value of using the arts as we mourn and grieve.

In navigating this book, you may progress in the order that the material has been arranged for you, or you may enter through the portal of one of the art chapters: Storytelling, Dancing, Music, Visual Arts. It is also possible to enter through the doorways of specific life experiences of grief: divorce and family estrangement, illness and aging, death and dying. Early on, whatever path you choose, I would point you to the chapter on loss and the many types of loss that are possible to experience, and to the chapter on The Grief Spiral.

Building on observations of the author C.S. Lewis in his work *A Grief Observed* and inspired by the reports of recent discoveries in neuroscience on the grieving brain, I've connected recent theories on grief, including the Dual Processing model, with the art images of spirals found in caves and burial sites in cultures all over the world. Exploring these connections provides support for why and how the arts can be powerful facilitators of our grieving processes and of their resolutions.

In short, art and art-making can help us to grieve. The best part? You don't have to be a skilled artist to realize the benefits. You do need a dose of willingness and courage to silence the inner negative voices of self-doubt. "I'm not creative." I can't carry a tune." "I have two left feet." Instead, all we need to allow the medicine of the arts to restore our souls is to follow our curiosity and allow it to connect with our creativity.

We'll challenge some preconceived, perhaps ill-conceived, notions about the famous "stages of grief." We'll look at how grief impacts our lives, whether we do it well or not. And I'll offer various ways we can use the arts to properly memorialize loss and gain new, healthy gifts from it.

In getting to a place of acceptance of grief as that which defines the human condition, we eliminate the taboos around issues of death and dying, grief and loss and bereavement that have affected our communal life for several generations. Once enough people embrace the realities of impermanence and unpredictability and learn something of what helps and what hinders the grieving process, my hope is we will find many other social problems on the way towards a solution as well. Loneliness might no longer be the number one public health epidemic across the globe with its impact on health being compared to smoking fifteen cigarettes a day. Anxiety may no longer be the number one mental health problem affecting forty million people a year. And once people embrace grief and grieving as an art worth getting good at, our enlivened energies will improve the quality of our individual lives and that of our collective communities as well.

Although progress has been made in the last few years regarding our culture's openness to learn about grief and to see death and other significant losses as a part of the human condition, there are still many miles to go, many discoveries to make about the importance of grief, and how the arts can inspire and instruct us in making grieving well the life-long art we need it to be. May you join me in using this book to help find those answers for you and those you love.

Part I
The Situation

"We are Un."

-*Sherman Alexie*

Chapter One

The Many Faces of Loss

I don't usually get my inspiration and key life lessons from bank regulators. But in that fateful year of 2020, Fed Chairman Jerome Powell got my attention with these words: "None of us has the luxury of choosing our challenges. Fate and history provide them for us." Like most everyone on the planet, in March of that year, the world and my life as I knew it shut down. At first, the loss meant a canceled presentation at a national conference I'd been looking forward to and having to postpone an airline trip to visit my granddaughter in California. The initial effect was not without some gains. Along with many of my friends and family members, the pause in the action got us off the unrelenting treadmill we'd been on, driven by our overcommitted calendars and too lengthy "to-do" lists. The loss of "business as usual" felt like a reprieve, but it didn't take long to realize that some of what had been interrupted might never return.

Do you remember where you were and what you were doing when you first got the news that a novel virus named Covid-19 had been identified and, ignoring national boarders, was spreading rapidly across the globe? Some deaths had already occurred, and no one knew its method of transmission. (Remember wiping down packages and grocery bags?) No one knew who or what would make someone vulnerable to the virus's attack.

Let's pause here and take a deep breath. I apologize for taking you back to that horrible time in our history—that time of isolation, fear, and uncertainty that most of us have emerged from. Much was interrupted. Most everyone experienced the loss of the familiar. Normal had to be redefined. What we did continue with, like grocery shopping, schooling, and work, had to be done in a different way. Looking back on it now, we see the loss of what we had expected to happen and what we had hoped to be doing in that period of our lives.

The need to grieve begins with loss. Seated in my dance studio in the lower level of my house, I looked at my computer screen and technology setup and gave myself a staunch talkin' to. "At your age, honey, you may never leave this room. If you want to keep doing any of what you've been doing, you must learn to do it through this little screen." And to my amazement, even now, I did. Taking back all the nasty things I had ever said or complained about regarding technology, I learned how to set up a media studio in my dance studio with lights, camera, and action! I became my own set designer, sound, and lighting technician, and began teaching classes, seeing clients on screen, and, best of all, having Zoom sessions with my granddaughter twice a week to help her and her parents with her online homeschooling.

It was the fear of dying, of spending my last hours of life in a hospital room on a respirator, isolated and alone, that motivated me to let go of the life I had known. No more moving about the country freely. I accepted this challenge that "fate and history" had handed me.

Like during other large-scale events that history and fate sometimes provide—wars, tornadoes, economic depressions—the impact of that three-year period of the worldwide pandemic **wasn't the same for everyone.** Everyone felt and experienced the impact of the pandemic differently, especially when it came to the isolation that it brought. Some people long for alone time while others view it as a punishment. This meant that the same types of losses affected people differently. If you had school-aged children whose schooling had to happen online from your kitchen table, were planning a wedding or a graduation ceremony, had an elderly loved one in a nursing home, or if you were an essential worker who had to leave your home and worry about bringing illness back to family members, you were likely treading water while trying to avoid the undertow. If you lost loved ones to death and had to say goodbye on an iPad screen and figure out how to hold a funeral over Zoom, or (God and Goddess forbid) you contacted the virus yourself and later had to live with *Long Covid*, you might rightly rate your pain to an over the top 15 on that pain scale healthcare providers are so fond of.

When the pandemic hit, it just so happened I had been writing and speaking for several years on the The Art of Grieving. I had already concluded that the number of losses in most people's ordinary lives coupled with the episodic nature of loss makes grieving a necessary skill that every human being needs to learn and become good at to have a rewarding life. Grieving is the internal processing of our thoughts and feelings related to loss. Mourning is the outward expression of that grief, which involves other people. By the year 2020, I had been using the performance arts of dancing, singing, and storytelling for many years to process the feelings generated by losses in my own life, and to help clients and students use various arts in processing their own. As I was in my studio, struggling to learn new technologies, I was surprised by something that happened, seemingly on its own, from a part of me I refer to as "that part that's smarter than I am."

A song from my childhood, popular during the Second World War, kept coming to me. A continually repeating ear worm I could not escape, its propelling rhythm continually repeated in my head, accompanying my every movement. "We did it before so we can do it again." I was amazed that I knew most of the words. Where is this coming from? What's the deal with this song?

Looking it up online, I learned that the song was popularized as a response to the attack on Pearl Harbor—a time when I would have been two to three years old; the time my mother first started me in dance classes. Did we dance to that song?

The song reminded people that, "We did it before," (we had made it through the First World War) and, "we can do it again." It became an anthem to inspire the nation to face the difficulties of war: separation from loved ones, rationing of gasoline and food—the difficulties that went on long enough that even now I still remember them.

Had I heard this song on the radio and marched around the house to its tune? Finding a cartoon of the song, it looked familiar. Little mouse characters marching and singing this message of encouragement in hard times. "We did it before. We can do it again." Could I have seen this on a newsreel in a movie theater? Whatever way it got into my brain, it became a soundtrack of needed encouragement for me in this present time.

Later, after I thought about it and wrote about it, I realized that some part of me, that "smarter than me part," made the connection to a song from long ago in my life, and created a reprieve to help me address what was happening in my present life. As I sat in wonder and awe at this gift, I realized another connection. It's been slightly over a century since the last worldwide pandemic (then called the 1918 Spanish Flu). The words and tune of the song work for that occasion as well. We made it through that pandemic, so we can make it through this one¬. A needed reminder that this pandemic, too, would end.

After all those challenges, and the long road it has been to "keep on keeping on" through them, our impulse, individually and collectively, is to put this all behind us and never speak of it again. That familiar gesture, brushing our fingers together while dusting off our palms to declare we're finished with a challenge, seems a universal cultural mudra. It's what our culture has been encouraging us to do regarding grief for at least the past century.

I recommend a different mudra, or position to take. Begin by naming a particular loss. Place the palms of your hands together in front of your chest as in the prayer pose and, as a martial arts practitioner bows to a worthy opponent, bow respectively to what is or has been your loss experience and the pain that is connected to it.

In offering beginning programs on The Art of Grieving online, it became apparent that people had not associated grieving with much else besides death. It felt important to increase our awareness of loss, to begin naming each loss and provide the opportunity to recognize it. In the online breakout rooms, I now call "connection rooms," I directed people to partner in an activity from InterPlay. Partner number one would say, "I could talk about..." and fill in the name of a loss they were currently experiencing. No details, just the name of it. The subject line of the email, not the details of the complete message.

Partner number two would say, "I could talk about..." and they would name a loss they were experiencing. The partners continued taking turns naming losses and staying present to hear their partner's list of losses. After a couple of minutes, I broadcasted further directions. "Now, take turns saying more about one of your losses. Fill in some details."

Returning everyone to the main room, I invited people to share in the chat box the type of losses they had come up with. People were surprised by how many kinds there were and how good it felt to simply recognize and name them. The pandemic had provided losses for most everyone but many losses they named had occurred before that experience, and some were ongoing. Some examples:

• My condo got mold last year and I lost art objects and possessions it had taken me years to collect.
• Contracting Lyme's disease took my energy and therefore put in jeopardy my ability to do the work I love.
• My mother's house fire destroyed all my childhood mementos.
• I had surgery to correct a problem it turns out I was born with, but now no more rich foods and favorite desserts.
• Not being able to celebrate family birthdays and graduations has been hard this past year.
• Working from home, I've lost the companionship of my co-workers, though I've picked up some time in not having to travel back and forth to the office.

After reading off the specific losses that the group came up with, I offered the categories of types of losses from the grief literature.

1. Anticipatory Loss – Sometimes we begin processing a loss before it occurs. Hearing rumors that the company may be downsizing, or waiting for the outcome of a loved one's medical test results may stimulate anticipatory grieving. During the pandemic, though people may have been managing their finances in the present, looming large was the fear of the future and what could happen in such uncertain times.

2. Secondary Loss – After an initial loss—when a parent dies or becomes unable to support their children—many secondary losses occur. Dependent family members may need to move, change schools, drop out and return to the job market, etc. All secondary losses result from the original one.

8

Like many elders in the country, my husband and I refrained from traveling and gathering in person with family members for the holidays. This was a primary loss of what had been our usual practice. It seemed more than a little odd that our children and grandchildren met and celebrated in our California house without us, while we stayed in Pittsburgh eating our holiday meal made for two. We watched on Zoom as family members opened their presents, and although this technology enabled us to observe the celebration, the feeling of disconnect and of being an outsider from the family community seemed to create a secondary loss.

3. Disenfranchised Loss – Sometimes we feel, or are made to feel by the culture, that our loss is not deserving of naming and grieving. It may be considered too trivial or small, or the relationship involved too distant to be relevant enough to deserve our grieving. As a culture, we appreciate the importance of the loss of a parent or a child, but we often overlook the impact of the death of a sibling, or a close friend from high school. We have few ceremonies or rituals to help people mourn a divorce, a job loss, or a serious business or career downturn. Community support is rarely available for a couple experiencing infertility or the loss of a child no one has gotten to know because the child died before or shortly after birth.

But it isn't a contest. The importance of a loss, the impact on an individual's sense of wellbeing or quality of life, does not follow genetic bloodlines or legal rules and regulations. The significance of the loss of a pet or a sibling, a friend or a stepparent, or a bankruptcy foreclosure may not be fully appreciated except by someone who has had their own similar experience or relationship to grieve.

4. Traumatic Loss – This is a loss that occurs suddenly and dramatically, "out of the blue," in circumstances unanticipated, sometimes due to an illegal activity or crime. One Monday morning, just before the lock down, my niece Heather, a single mom of two teenage boys and a fifth-grade teacher in Nevada, sent the following group text message to members of our far-flung family.

"...Jacob died in his sleep Sunday night,
apparently drug related though we
don't know the exact cause of death yet."

Glancing at my phone sent my heart racing, my lungs could only afford short sips of breath, as I imagined being with Heather and eighteen-year-old son Jacob, who was set to join the Marines a few months after graduation. Wishing I could put my arms around her, my mind and heart went out to the millions of families who received such news flashing onto their devices in the last few years. This escape to the awareness of others reduced my sense of isolation, but it increased my sense of horror and overpowering helplessness.

"I will let you know of
any services planned...
There is lots of support here.
But sad days are ahead."

I sent a return text.

"Aunt Sheila here–
Oh, Dear One!
As someone who has felt
the sad days ahead that you

10

are referring to, I wrap you
round with infinite love
and wisdom. Call when you
get a minute to talk."

She did call the next day and I learned that Jacob had been celebrating the Super Bowl victory of his favorite team with friends the night before by using a recreational drug, even though they had had a mutual friend die of an overdose a few days before. Later, we learn that the recreational drug had been laced with fentanyl, which caused his death—the fourth teenage student from the same high school. As a popular teacher, Heather would have students and colleagues looking to her to organize the community's response to be able to shelter other students from a repeat involvement with this evil epidemic.

5. **Ambiguous Loss** – In relating to a friend or loved one who is experiencing one of the versions of dementia, the situation is ambiguous for you and for that person as well. The person is still alive but their ability to function and relate to others is impacted and, in many cases, the relationship is diminished dramatically.

I visited my sister Pat every six months in Boston where she was living in a facility due to her Alzheimer's disease. In between visits, I talked with her on the phone weekly. When Covid hit, she, like all the other residents in facilities around the country, was unable to have visitors. Due to the stress and overwhelm of her professional caregivers, we couldn't connect frequently, and I worried she would not be able to recognize me. It brought me great joy one day when an aide was able to hold the iPad for a call and I heard Pat say, "That looks like my sister," in a voice that suggested she couldn't understand what my face was doing on that tiny screen. I was delighted that she still knew my face.

11

6. Cumulative Losses – The pandemic has done us one favor. It has dispelled forever any expectation that important losses will occur singularly and in some sort of orderly fashion, like completing third grade before you move to fourth grade. It's also part of how grieving works that. In the process of grieving a single loss, memories of previous losses and ways we dealt with them can be stimulated and unearthed, compounding the complexity of processing the present one. These **cumulative losses** may overwhelm us at times, while also offering the opportunity to process the earlier losses further.

7. Non-Finite Losses – Sometimes called **Living Losses** or **Chronic Sorrows,** these are losses that will endure for the rest of a person's life, continuing to cause their life to fall short of what had been expected. A chronic and deteriorating disease such as Parkinson's, Multiple Sclerosis, or Lou Gehrig's Disease are examples since cures and disease management practices have not yet improved enough to bring noteworthy relief.

8. Loss of Identity – Many losses have other losses tucked inside them, hidden from first view. The loss of a job isn't just about money or a steady income. We often identify ourselves and one another through the work we do in the world. Certain jobs ensure our place in society, many structure our lifestyle. It's about the routine and structure in the day, the social interactions that cluster around the main assignment, and the self-identity and social position that the title bestows. The importance of each of these elements varies with the type of job, the length of tenure in the position, and the years of preparation leading up to acquiring it.

Many losses alter how we see ourselves and how others see us. For example, whether through divorce or death of one's partner, the identity of being a part of a couple and connecting socially with other couples ends. When our parents die, we become orphans. When a child dies, whether as an adult or while still in their youth, the parents lose the future they had expected to be able to witness and live.

9. Loss of Cultural Identity – Whether manmade or natural, changes in the environment are creating a loss of identity in many cultures and communities. The author Sherman Alexie wrote how the construction of the Grand Coulee Dam impacted his northwestern Native American community. His people had been known as the Salmon People, as salmon were central to their way of life, diet, and sustenance. Once the dam interfered with the salmon's life cycle, there were no more salmon. Alexie wrote how his people's identity changed:

> "Our identity has been clarified for us.
> We are the unsalmon people.
> We are unsalmon.
> We are un."

Affirming what Alexie wrote about his community, Laurie, a dancer friend, and member of my Pittsburgh community, reported back to us six months after she returned to Alaska for her second tour of teaching native children there. The difference in the community from the previous year was dramatic. Two Thousand and Nineteen was the first year that salmon had to be flown in due to the drought caused by global warming. There was no salmon for members of the community to catch, prepare, package, and share, which meant that the social life involved with all these activities was gone as well. Describing the adults in the community, Laurie used the words "depressed" and "demoralized." "It was like they were sleepwalking, leaving the children to fend for themselves." The dedication and love that Laurie had brought to teaching dance and art to the elementary school children was no match for the overwhelming losses and their effects on the community. Out of self-compassion and the need for self-care, she made the hard decision to not renew her teaching contract for the following year.

As a country, we are experiencing a tsunami of losses. Over a million lives lost during the two years of the pandemic— about as many deaths as occurred during World War II, but these deaths happened in far less time. And like during a war, the casualties have not been spread equally throughout the population. The elderly and minority communities have been hit much harder. The pandemic has caused many of our societal systems to crash. We lost half a million healthcare providers who resigned or retired from their jobs to recover from burnout and hopefully find less stressful work. At this writing, it's unclear how we will replace them. Some say, rather than try, we should accept that the system is broken and design one that focuses on keeping all our people healthy and out of the hospital.

Another half million teachers have left the classroom; some say to enter the business world where they'll get better pay and shorter hours. When teachers need a second job to survive, is it time to rethink education? We're still not done counting the losses and costs to our children's mental health and educational progress. We are full of questions without answers as we look into the future.

You've probably heard the popular phrase, "Everyone grieves differently." As a grief advocate, I'm concerned this might be misleading. While it's true that each episode of grieving, even for the same person, has its own flavor, it's important for us to be able to exchange compassionate understanding with one another and learn from one another, no matter the differences.

14

Admittedly, it's complicated. And popular Western culture doesn't like complicated or complex and has lots of trouble with nuance. While it's important to recognize that each loss is unique as is each episode of the grieving that accompanies it, similar factors operate to make that uniqueness.

1. How did the news of the loss get delivered? Our response to a loss is strongly affected by how we learn of the loss. Consider the differences if you stumble across the news on social media or your workday is interrupted abruptly by a vibration from your cell phone. What if you walk into a room and discover a loved one is no longer alive, or you are physically present for much of their dying process? What if a work colleague tells you that your job has been given to someone else, or you hear that the company you work for is being acquired? The element of surprise and the amount of time you have to prepare will greatly impact the timing and intensity of your grieving process.

2. What is the relationship one had with the person who died, and how dependent is the mourner is on them? The age of a child when they lose a parent matters, not only to the immediate effect, but throughout the years when the missing still occurs, and continues throughout the years, noticeable on every landmark life occasion. Fear and uncertainty about the future are often prominent when a widow or widower must now raise children alone without the financial and emotional support of a partner.

3. What kind of support has the person had while experiencing the loss and grieving it? The emotional weight can be shared if someone else is around to bear the burden, after the casserole dishes are returned. The experience

15

is totally different if there is no ritual, or you weren't invited, and you've been left alone to find your own answers.

4. What was the nature of the relationship at the time of the loss? The emotional severity can often be related to how much emotional equity you invested in the relationship. Consider these: if you've been out of touch for years and you hear about the death weeks later, or you had a disagreement with the person shortly before they died, or since there was no communal support for the relationship, there are no co-mourners.

5. How did the person die and what was the length of the process? Journeying with a loved one through a long illness can make exhaustion a central feature of the support person's initial recovery. If death comes out of the blue, with no warning, or if the cause could be seen in retrospect as preventable, the smorgasbord of possible emotions is enormous. What if the death occurs because of a crime, or from actions taken by an officer of the law?

6. What else was going on in the person's life at the time? Ongoing circumstances impact our grief. For example, your job loss happens just after you've purchased a new home, this is your third miscarriage, the death of your partner leaves you penniless, or you have experienced four deaths of people close to you in the last twelve months.

7. What's going on in the larger world? It was hard to count, let alone deal with, all the losses the shutdown and isolation of the pandemic created or exacerbated. As our changing climate is fueling more intense and frequent floods and fires, whole communities are being impacted. And hearing about one more mass shooting at the mall or in a school can feel like the last straw.

These factors and more have left people of all ages with a nearly overwhelming number of losses to grieve, and losses to expect in the future. Since the recent years of the global pandemic, when every person on the planet was and may still be suffering multiple losses, it is time to embrace grief as something we need to get good at and see what learning to do it well offers for our future lives.

When all is said and done, the most important factor that affects our processing of our losses comes down to our attitude about loss itself. If we interpret loss as something to avoid at all costs, as a personal failure, or something that shouldn't be happening, we create more suffering for ourselves and others.

In working with an organization of nuns, dealing with the multiple organizational and individual losses that have plagued their communities for the past twenty years or so, I was introduced to another way.

I was gathered with four sisters around a large round table at their motherhouse. Our task was to plan a celebration to honor the anniversary of the 150 years the community had been in the United States. We noted, in this long view, the many losses and dramatic changes the sisters have had to navigate throughout this long history, beginning with the trip from their homeland in Europe.

One of the sisters shared a community ritual that they had been using recently whenever a significant loss was about to be experienced by the community. Whether the loss is expected or unanticipated, gradual or sudden, small or mammoth, they ask this same question out loud in community and repeat it quietly to themselves. They follow it with a meditation to listen for its answers. The question: "To what **life** is **this loss** calling us?"

After the sisters told me about this ritual, I thought about losses in my own life, situations in which things turned out very differently than I had intended or wished for—a move I did not want, a divorce, a job termination, the death of my children. How much ease might this question have brought me had I known enough to ask it?

I began sharing the ritual with others, and it seemed to help people tune into the intuitive part of their minds, the "part that is smarter than we are." Rather than staying in a bad mood over the fact that things have not turned out the way we expected or planned, by asking and then listening for an answer, we allow for the possibility that something good could come from a particular circumstance. It seems to help us take a longer view, allowing for the notion that something good could happen in what the sisters call, "God's timing."

My thirty-one-year-old grandson, Ethan, and I were talking about how many things must come together for a person to even get born. He reminded me of some family history. "Grandpa was in a very serious automobile accident before my dad was born. The people in the front seat died, and his recovery took a long time. If he hadn't been sitting in the backseat, my dad wouldn't be here, and neither would my sister, brother, and me." I mentioned, too, a couple of close calls in the forms of icy roadways and totaled cars that his mother had survived before she became their mother.

It didn't surprise me that Ethan would reflect on such an important concept since I remembered what happened in their family when he and his brother were five and three years old. Their mother lost twins at twelve weeks and the boys had gone through excitement and sadness over that loss, then excitement again when a year or so later their sister Tori was born. It became a kind of family ritual that whenever I drove the boys past the cemetery where the twins were buried, they would call out to them, "Hi twins." One day, six-year-old Ethan's reflective voice came from the backseat, "You know, if the twins hadn't died, we wouldn't have Tori."

It takes stepping back for a longer view to recognize that fate and history have a part to play in our lives, and to trust that there is no such thing as a life without loss, nor a loss that, once grieved, will not lead us to a gift or gain.

Artist Resource

In the first year of the pandemic, when my colleague Christine and I were teaching Radical Self-Care classes online, we discovered the work of an amazing composing and performing husband and wife duo, Abigail and Shaun Bengson. Their storytelling set to music was performed with audio and video and recorded in their home during the pandemic lockdown. When we were wondering if or when Covid would ever end, their song "The Keep Going Song" became a soundtrack for our lives, spurring us on—and on, and on. Since many aspects of grieving often take longer than we want them to, this song may help you keep going on, too, when you hit one of those unrelenting, seemingly stalled places on your life path.

Reflection/Action

1. Find a partner to try out the activity my students and I did, taking turns naming losses. "I could talk about..." After a minute or so of exchanges, partner #1 should say more about one of their losses. Then partner #2 should do the same.

19

2. Now share what stands out for you now about loss and how it feels to recognize and name your losses.

3. One of the most comprehensive resource books on grief is Eleanor Haley and Litsa Williams' *What's Your Grief?* Its subtitle describes its format: *Lists to Help You Through Any Loss.* Check out the list of Existential Questions Prompted by Loss on pages 148-150.

4. Select one of your losses and ask the sisters' question, "To what life is this loss calling me?" Don't forget to allow time for an answer.

Chapter Two

Navigating the Grief Spiral

A well-known literary figure of the twentieth century, C.S. Lewis wrote his reflections of his own bereavement process when he lost the love of his life, his wife, Joy Davidman. *A Grief Observed* was published in 1961 under the pseudonym N.W. Clerk because Lewis wished to avoid the connection with his other work, which may tell us much about the unpopularity or taboo of the topic. We are fortunate that he wrote it, giving us a personal description of his own experience of grief, sharing what I believe to be elements of a universal model. "For in grief nothing 'stays put.' One keeps on emerging from a phase, but it always recurs. Round and round, everything repeats. Am I going in circles, or dare I hope I am on a spiral?"

What is this spiral that Lewis is hoping for as he observes his own grieving process? It can't be what people mean when they refer to themselves or someone else as "spiraling out of control." The pattern of negative thoughts which trigger more negative thoughts into a downward spiral of declining moods or mental illness seems way worse than his fear of making no progress, of "going in circles." As he is processing the loss of his wife, a partner he found later in his life, and having to let go of her sooner than either of them expected or wanted, Lewis hopes he is on a spiral path of growth and insight. His hope would have been well placed because he was likely familiar with the concept of the spiral. Found in cultures worldwide, the spiral is one of the oldest intuitive symbols of the physical, mental, and spiritual development of a human life as it winds its way through the seasons of its years.

Spirals are found in every aspect of nature. The growth spiral or logarithmic spiral is seen in the unfurling of fern leaves, the shape of snail shells, the arrangement of flower pedals, the cochlea of the inner ear. Spirals are patterns that occur naturally in plants and nature's systems, including the weather and the spiraling galaxy of the Milky Way. Not just a simple circle, the path of a spiral changes levels as it grows or moves in time and space. Rotating water forms multi-level wave patterns in the surf as does, on a smaller scale, water exiting a drain. In his book, *Spirals: The Pattern of Existence*, poet, journalist, and musician Geoff Ward calls the spiral "the eternal sign of the creative and organizing principle at work in the universe." In the science of nature, the spiral shape and path are how the life force energy moves. In the search for evidence of a divine creator, the spiral as a form is ascribed symbolic and sacred meanings in what is known as Sacred Geometry. It is found in the architecture of cathedrals, temples, mosques and other places of worship, intent on connecting people to larger realities.

Grief is the processing of our life experiences to determine what to cherish and hold dear and what to let go of that will no longer serve us and the person we become in the future. For this, we need to be continually gaining new perspectives related to loss. Lewis notes what every mourner throughout the ages has likely noted: "everything moves around," and, "nothing stays put." So, grieving is clearly not a linear stepping-stoned procedure. Seeing grieving as a spiral rather than the navigation of stairsteps or stages, or a timeline, or a circle offers reassurance and guidance to make sense out of what is often experienced as incomprehensible and overwhelming.

Representing the cycle of the seasons and the cycles of life, growth, and change, the spiral brings us back to the same place each season but on a more evolved level, offering new perspectives with each turn. The anniversary of the loss occurs, but the mourner now has had another year of living without their beloved, and they are viewing the situation from a different vantage point.

I recently experienced a loss that renewed my perspective and totally stretched my expectation of how many years and for how many turns of the spiral, with its evolving levels, might this process still operate. The death was of my former husband George. It was a few days after his ninety-third birthday. We had married sixty-one years prior to his death and had been divorced for forty-seven.

When I got the news, his death was expected, though no one can accurately predict the time of someone's coming into this life or leaving it. It was not a tragic death. George had a long and productive life. Once it's clear there is no turning back, no recovering and feeling better, the work for the person is to get out of this life, to let go of it, and for those who love them to support that process. A few minutes after my former husband achieved this, my son called to tell me. I expressed my sorrow, but also my joy that his work and his suffering were finished. The following morning however, I awoke with a deep sense of sorrow—a sorrow I could not comprehend.

By now, I know the drill. Stay with the feeling. Honor the sorrow and let it speak to you. In a short while, my memory spiraled me back to the sorrow I felt when George and I divorced. I've heard it said that we are still, in some way, all the ages we have ever been, so I recognized this sorrow as belonging to that twenty-two-year-old young woman I was, so full of the courage and convictions that love bestows — the woman who had said the words and made the promise "until death do us part." Now, she and I were experiencing the sorrow that we didn't get to fulfill that promise. After sharing this with my online women's group and receiving their support, I felt what seemed a final resolution to that chapter of my life.

It is well accepted and understood in the grief literature that grieving does not and should not take place alone. The support of my women's group helped me complete another turn on my own Grief Spiral. This type of communal grief work is often represented in the visual arts of our ancestors.

Visual motifs of the spiral are some of the oldest images of human art. The original artwork of spiral designs date from 3200 BCE and can be found on the entrance stone at the Megalithic Passage Tomb at Newgrange in Ireland. Looking closely with the aid of a graphic overlay, we see that the multiple spirals that cover the stone are placed side by side, often touching one another, and sometimes, their spiraling lines flow into one another, indicating connection. The need for support through grieving was a given among the early peoples, and a wisdom that modern day research confirms. Those people who receive support for their grieving, particularly in the early phases, are more likely to eventually achieve a positive resolution.

When I was grieving the loss of my son Kenneth, I used an improvisational form to tell of a particular experience that I had had with him when he was dying. The form is called "the gesture choir" and requires the teller to use exaggerated gestures in their telling, while several members, the "choir," stand behind and imitate the teller's movements. I like to call this form the "we've got your back" form because that's how it feels when you are the teller. It came to me during the telling that *some stories are too big for one body to hold* — an ancient truth that I was rediscovering.

Given that the appearance of the spiral is found throughout the world across time and location, some anthropologists speculate a connection to the human brain, specifically the visual cortex. Learning that the universality of the spiral image across cultures likely came from early peoples' visual experiences, I connected immediately to what I was learning about the grieving brain. In reading neuroscientist and psychologist Mary-Frances O'Connor's book, *The Grieving Brain: The Surprising Science of How We Learn from Love and Loss,* I realized that the brain itself operates as a kind of spiral. It must change its structure, rewire itself to account for the reality that someone who was, what O'Connor calls "here, now and close," no longer is. The mourner may, even weeks after the funeral, experience moments when they expect their deceased loved one to walk in the back door, returning from work as they had done for many years. People report dialing their phone to share with a deceased friend something they know their friend would appreciate hearing about. Joan Didion describes this illogical response in her book *The Year of Magical Thinking,* written after the death of her husband. Months after his death, she found herself unable to give her husband's slippers away. She told herself, "He might need them when he returns."

O'Connor turns to Lewis and his description of his experience of this disconnect as an illustration of how the grieving brain works. "Thought after thought, feeling after feeling, action after action, had [my wife] for their object. Now that target is gone... so many roads lead thought to [her]. So many roads once; now so many cul-de-sacs."

What keeps these spirals, these experiences of cul-de-

25

sacs, from becoming the negative experience of "spiraling out of control?" Many mourners question themselves when such "foolish," "nonsensical," "crazy" thoughts and feelings occur. "What's the matter with me? I must be losing my mind." Or people worry that a loved one must be "losing *their* mind." But knowing how grieving works in the brain can turn those questions and negative self-talk into a flash of recognition, giving it coherent meaning. "There it is again, my magical thinking."

Such a response illustrates one of two aspects in the process of grieving: the one where we consciously, intellectually *do* the grieving. Grieving becomes an art when we explore thoughts that help us make sense of our experience. It matters what we say to ourselves. We may ask, "Why me?" then sooner or later realize this is not a helpful question. Changing it to, "Why *not* me?" offers a different perspective, one where we recognize ourselves as being part of events and processes that affect the entire human family.

Having educated ourselves about grieving, rather than being captured by the pattern of negative self-talk—a negative spiral of "I must be going crazy," or, "I'm insane," or, "I've lost myself and the reasonable person I used to be," —we can say, "There it is, my brain's doing that *magical thinking* thing again!"

The second aspect of processing loss involves the subconscious processing that continuously takes place throughout our grief, outside of our awareness. Just as our bodies, outside of our awareness, process the food that we eat so that it is available to nourish our cells, and process and eliminate the waste products from our digestive process, our intuitive, dreamtime consciousness is continually processing our life experiences. Our part in this is to decide to put ourselves in situations where grief can work its magic.

Despite cultural or family programming, we know now

the importance of expressing our feelings, especially our sorrow. So, arrange time and situations for that to happen. We soak in a hot tub and allow the steaming relaxation to encourage our tears. By the time the water has gotten cold, our feelings and thoughts have changed, and that episode of sorrow will have come to a resolution, for now. Or we write or talk about our experiences, letting whatever emerges be released on the page, or in the presence of a respectful witness, and we get what my friend Rose said happens to her: "I finally know what I think when I hear myself say it out loud."

We put ourselves in a place for grief to work its magic when we use the arts to help us process our lives. In the episodic life-long process of grieving as an art itself, we use the arts of music, poetry, dance, storytelling, and visual arts as portals to take us into liminal space—that space indigenous peoples call the space "between the worlds." We express and celebrate and create through writing, chanting, drawing, dancing, cooking, gardening, making masks, helping others (or rejoicing in those people who are helping others), transforming pain into compassion, loss into the commitment to helping the world become a better place in honor of our loved one having been in it. And, after a period of mourning, we find the courage to recommit to life and to love again.

I was at the neighborhood Verizon store, selecting a decorative cover for my new phone. A version of the iconic Japanese woodblock print of waves was offered as one of the choices. I had been looking for an image that could represent grieving and provide a way to think about it. Checking my own somatic response to the image, I thought to myself, "Yes, that's an image of what grief is like." Later, when I searched for larger images of the print, I found the work even more illustrious of my grief experiences. As I studied the image of the waves, it became clear they were being moved by winds and storms

27

from larger forces. In the varying heights of the surf, I noted small boats containing groupings of people navigating the turbulent waters together. For me, this represented how our individual grief takes place in our families and communities, and how it, too, is affected by larger realities. Meditating on this print, my focus went to the boats, imagining that those aboard some of the boats are paddling together with a synchronous rhythm, while in others, the group is in disarray, perhaps struggling to throw one of their boatmates overboard into the swirling sea. When the sea is calm, when the sorrow becomes sweet sorrow, the travelers enjoy the smooth motion of the gentle sea. But the time will come again when they need to marshal all their individual and communal strength to stay the course of their individual and collective journeys, to not be overcome by the intensity and frequency of the waves.

Water streams moving in two different directions are forced to turn and swirl around each other, forming a spiraling whirlpool. When a loved one dies, there can be a desire, a wish, to go with them. And an opposite desire to bring them to where we are.

My son died early in the morning on the summer solstice. His boyfriend, Les, had gone home, but not before he had me promise to notify him when Kenneth crossed. So, of course, I did. I left a message on what I thought was his phone's voicemail. I felt awful when I found out that I had mixed up his personal and business phone numbers, and my message went to the one he didn't check until morning. But Les told me not to feel bad. It turned out this mistake gave him the opportunity to have a most amazing experience.

"Ken came to me in a dream," Les said. "He looked terrific, happy, energetic, and healthy. He didn't have AIDS and cancer anymore. He said, 'Come with me,' but I told him I couldn't do that."

28

The following morning, Les was in a car accident that completely totaled his new car. He walked away unscathed from the accident site. But hearing both segments of his story gave me chills because I was familiar with the notion that the recently bereaved are more at risk for dying themselves than at other times in their lives.

Bringing Les into our lives was most satisfying when we held Ken's memorial service a few days later. His friends, many who had performed with him in the theatre, and family members filled the large room with towering bouquets of flowers, inspiring music, and stories and songs of Ken and their love for him. His college theatre teacher provided a video of his performance in the musical Oliver. We heard and saw a twenty-something Ken sing and dance at his own memorial, "Consider yourself at home. Consider yourself one of the family."

When the event ended, I told my husband, "I never want to leave this room. It is so full of love; every molecule of air is filled with it." His response to me, which I will never forget, no matter how long my own life will be, was, "Well, that's where Ken is now."

In our grieving processes, from the earliest days throughout many years beyond, we alternate between tending to the business of our own lives and reaching back and remembering those that we have loved and lost. If we know this can happen automatically and unexpectedly when something in an environment stimulates our memory of a loved one, we again avoid an incident of spiraling into negative self-talk. As we move out into a world that does not contain our loved one, it is full of things that remind us of them, bringing us back to the person and our loss. Again, "nothing stays in place." What we thought was finished isn't.

A nun told me of being overcome suddenly by feelings of grief in the aisle of a grocery store. Another sister, a friend she had lived in community with for many years, had died six months previously. The community's rituals, a celebration of the sister's life, a funeral in the chapel of the motherhouse, and burial in the community cemetery had all been done as they are for every sister who has given her life to the noble purposes of her religion and community. But here was this nun, flooded by memories of her dearly departed friend, and the feelings attached to them, in the middle of a sunny fall afternoon.

Reaching for a tissue, she looked about the store, totally perplexed by what was happening to her. "I noticed I was in the bakery section, where mince meat pies were displayed on a nearby table. My friend loved baking, and mince meat pies were her specialty," she told me. I tried to offer some support by letting her know that there is a name for such incidents — they are called "Grief Bursts." Technically, the scent of the pies connected her with her loved one by stimulating chemicals in her body that produced emotions that lasted six seconds. In the following ninety seconds, according to brain scientist Dr. Jill Bolte Taylor, the sensations became feelings as she began to make meaning of her emotional reaction. The sister's brain, stimulated by the smell of a scent, connected her back to her friend and her loss.

You've probably had the experience of being unsettled or troubled about something, then taking a walk, and either during the walk or shortly after it, having a solution present itself. I understand this phenomenon to be that the movement of the walk interrupts the conscious intellectual linear thought patterns, and allows another part of our brain, the intuitive part, the "time out of time" part, to gift us with a heart-centered idea or perspective. Walking the spiral path of the labyrinth is such an action.

30

The practice of walking a type of spiral path dates to some 4000 years ago in what is now Southern Europe. Versions of spiral paths are found in ancient Crete, Italy, France, Norway, India, among Hopi Native Americans, and in the British Isles. It is an ancient practice used by persons of different religious faiths and those of no faith to alter the state of the walker's mind. It encourages meditation, mind-body states of centering and grounding, and self-reflection in order to gain insight.

Twenty years ago, during the time I was a caregiver for my daughter who was undergoing a bone marrow transplant at MD Anderson in Houston, I was a presenter at a Spirituality and Social Work Conference in Austin. As a kind of bonus activity, the conference organizers had set up an indoor canvas version of a spiraling labyrinth in a gymnasium space in the building where the conference was being held. I knew that labyrinths offer the opportunity for quieting the mind, encouraging meditation, and enhancing creativity, so after I did my presentation, I set out to walk the labyrinth. Walking on the single winding path from the outer edge that takes one on a circuitous path, I was at times advancing, at times retreating, but eventually the path took me to the center. In that space, I paused for several minutes. As the instructions suggested, I let go of the responsibility for my daughter's wellbeing that I had been carrying—as her mother and her caregiver. "I surrender my daughter Corinne into the hands of God." Saying this to myself brought tears to my eyes at the time, as it does now as I type these words.

Then, exiting the spiral, I walked the same path out as I had walked coming in. The moment my feet left the canvas surface, and I felt the cool wooden gymnasium floor on the bottom of my feet, I heard a voice say, "*We* are the hands of God."

All the people who had been helping my daughter and her family by delivering meals, carpooling the children to sports practices and games, and the friends who stood in for me when I needed respite as Corinne's caregiver came to my mind. I saw their smiling faces and felt a feeling of the deepest gratitude, which underlined the truth of the message I had just heard.

Seeing grieving as a spiral, we are not left to figure life out by ourselves. We see ourselves and the losses and changes our lives bring us as part of a natural process with eons of experience behind it. Knowing that grief is non-linear, we can rely on the fact that our intuitive mind is built to process it. There is a part of us that is "smarter than we are," and putting ourselves in spaces and places where our spiraling brain allows us to access that inner wisdom, we gain the many gifts of grief.

Rather than seeing grieving as our culture had for the last hundred years as something to fear, avoid, postpone, or when engaged in, to be done quickly, we savor grief's gifts. We appreciate the compassion for others in the same boat that sparks in us gratitude for our own life and those we have shared it with. We appreciate the gift of connection to "all that is," to "all our relations," as the Native American cultures express it. We appreciate grief's gift of purpose where, in honoring those we love, we take actions to make the world a better place for our loved one having been in it.

Artist Resource

In walking the path of the grief spiral, loved ones who have gone from our sight hold memories of who we were in an earlier time, and images of who we are becoming.

In some cultures, to honor and stay connected to their ancestors, people construct shrines in their homes. One of my mentors, Cynthia Winton-Henry, in addition to being a dancer and the author of *The Art of Ensoulment: A Playbook on How to Create from Body and Soul,* is a shrine artist. She creates small memorials to commemorate important people and times in her life. She suggests that "if you've ever put flowers on a grave, placed a photo of a deceased family member in a prominent place in your home, made an altar with found objects, or displayed your loved one's memorabilia in a box, you are a shrine-maker already."

From this perspective, I created a shrine when I put a statue of two young girls that my sister had given me years ago in the garden outside my office window. Looking up from my desk, I am reminded of her and sweet memories of us as sisters. Cynthia defines shrines and their purpose this way: "Like soul collage, shrine-making is an active, creative way to center our everyday and transcendent connection to death. With life and emotions rapidly speeding by, a shrine can be a holy stopping place to bow, reflect, and connect, even for a moment."

Reflection/Action

1. Look around the room where you are. Are their objects or items that belonged to a deceased loved one or that remind you of them? If so, what do you experience when focusing on them? If there are no items, can you imagine something that, though not physically present, reminds you of them?

2. Like what happened to the nun in the grocery store aisle, have you ever had the experience of a sudden "Grief Burst"? Were you able to identify the source that stimulated it?

3. What images represent the grieving process for you? Experiment with drawing a diagram of how you experience grief.

Chapter Three

Culture and Emotions: The Water We Swim In

It seems an almost universal response. The person is asked about something negative that has happened: "How is your mother doing?" or, "What do you remember about the accident?" or, "Was she your only sister?" Next, as the person begins to talk about the situation, their voice begins to quiver, or they may begin to tear up—all examples of "losing their composure." It only takes a few seconds for the person to look embarrassed and begin apologizing, "Oh, I'm so sorry."

When my sister-in-law asked me about my son who was in the hospital, I saw this response in reverse. As I began describing his situation, I teared up a bit. This prompted an immediate apologetic response from her. "I'm so sorry. Now I've *made* you cry."

Standing back a bit from these familiar reactions, we can conclude that Western culture's rules for human conduct in adverse situations, though often unstated, are versions of "Keep calm and carry on," and, "Whatever you do, don't become *emotional*."

From the perspective of processing our life experiences and grieving our losses, these cultural "rules" are the direct opposite of what we need to grieve. On the path of good grieving, we must be able to recognize, accept, and express our emotions. And to be good companions to our loved ones as they grieve, we must be able to allow them to have and express their feelings in our presence. Therapists, grief experts, and teachers in the grief field have several pithy ways to express this truth: "Grieving requires witnesses," and, "You have to *feel* it to heal it," and "The way out is through."

There are multiple reasons why we have trouble processing our own grief and supporting others who are processing theirs. First, emotional literacy is not a given in Western culture for people of any age. Classroom teachers attempt to teach it by asking children, "How are you feeling today?" while displaying a chart of emoji faces labeled with specific emotions. I've been familiar with versions of this chart of emotions for years, but I'm still amazed at the number of choices that exist. Going for simplicity, I often focus on a short list of the basics—mad, sad, glad, scared, and disgusted. Emotions are the raw data, the sensations in our body that give us information about our present reality.
A key part of my life's work has been finding ways to help people get in and stay in their bodies so they can be present for their life. Living life in this embodied way gives us the ability to identify what we are experiencing. To the body, feelings are just sensations, comfortable or uncomfortable, until we give them names. For grieving to become the art we need it to be, we must be *in* our bodies to *have* our feelings rather than our feelings *having* us.

Danger and difficulties related to grief occur when a person is unaware that they are grieving, and their disowned or ignored feelings take over, their life running amuck. "I don't know what's the matter with me," a client might say. "I yelled at my son this morning," or, "I couldn't get out of bed," or, "I went into the boss's office to discuss the matter and, before I knew it, I had quit my job." Avoiding such dysfunctional situations is what the resilience literature calls "emotional regulation."

Regulation of our emotions is made more difficult because cultures and subcultures have "rules" about who can express emotions and when and how. This causes some emotions to hide behind a more "approved" one or causes people to get stuck in an emotion that does not serve them. This is evident most commonly with anger and sadness. I remember a client coming to me complaining of her inability to stop crying. "I've been crying for a week, and I can't stop," she told me. As she sat listless in the chair, telling her story in a soft, whiney voice, I learned that her husband was divorcing her and, to get total custody of their children, he tricked her into leaving the house long enough to change the locks and file papers that claimed she had abandoned them. Possession is nine-tenths of the law.

Listening to her story, I felt my own anger rising inside me and I asked her, "Do you ever get mad?" She said no, and I saw that without her anger she was helpless. I asked her to imagine what her husband's reaction would have been had she done to him what he did to her. No surprise. She told me he'd get so angry, he'd get a gun and come after her.

In my husband's family, no one was allowed to be angry except their father, who made the rule. In my family, everyone expressed anger, which often hid other feelings of hurt, shame, fear, or betrayal. When this idea came up during an online session, my friend Laverne shared a popular meme from her Facebook page: "I sat with my anger long enough till she told me her real name is Grief."

The second challenge to identifying and expressing our feelings is the way in which Western culture has shamed tears, which can be the expression of many feelings, but particularly sadness and sorrow. Most everyone is familiar with the restrictions on tears that boys and men are raised with— "Boys don't cry." So, men of course can't either, and since it's "unladylike" to express anger, many girls and women are unpracticed in being able to assert themselves. For most everybody of any age, tears are for "crybabies," and people are admonished to "stop feeling sorry for yourself." Tears, if considered appropriate at all, are to happen only in the privacy of one's own home.

My parents, when they were raising six kids in the 1940s and 50s, took this one step further. There was only one appropriate space for crying in our house and it was the bathroom. If one of us began to cry, we were sent there to remove ourselves from the company of other family members and only allowed back into the family living spaces when we were calm and collected. If your family had any version of such restrictions, small wonder we end up apologizing for expressing our own sorrows in social situations.

Much of what Western culture has taught us about grief and the grieving process is not so. The predominant model for grieving, still repeated in news articles, conversations, and online is the image of grief as a series of orderly stair steps through predictable emotional stages where we arrive at a completion that puts it all behind us. We individually climb those stairs, and arriving at the top landing, we dust off our palms and declare victory. We have arrived. We have conquered our grief, and it is finished. We can now move on with our lives. And when this is not so, we tell ourselves, "There's something wrong with me."

As a mental health professional working with hundreds of individuals and families for over thirty years, I know this model to be a cause of much suffering. Its author, physician

Elizabeth Kubler-Ross, did not intend her observations of dying patients grieving their own impending deaths in a hospice setting to be generalized and applied to all people grieving all kinds of losses. The orderly stages we expect to find do not exist, though some of the feelings described certainly do. In her book, *On Death and Dying*, Kubler-Ross put quotation marks around the word "stages" to avoid exactly what our culture has done with her work—making it prescriptive and causing us to judge ourselves and others harshly when our grieving process doesn't match this model.

After a life that has given me many opportunities to grieve, allow me to suggest that the five "stages" in this model could be considered five emotions or thoughts that can and do occur, sometimes repeatedly throughout the process of grieving a particular loss and the secondary losses that often accompany them. It's important to note, however, that Kubler-Ross's list does not contain two emotions central to grief itself: sadness and, it's more intense form, sorrow.

I like to think of these emotions—denial, anger, bargaining, depression, acceptance—as a short list of emotional possibilities, some of the eighty-seven varieties social work researcher Brené Brown has identified in her research.

I've become acquainted with a myriad of other emotions surrounding my own grief from every time I meet someone new and they ask how many children I have. When I give a fully truthful answer—that I had three children: a middle son Kevin who lives in California, our youngest son Kenneth who died of AIDs at thirty-one years of age, and our daughter Corinne who died of breast cancer at forty-two—I can feel a huge gulf begin to develop between us as we become surrounded by a sea of awkwardness. The entire interaction often leaves me feeling excluded from communities of ordinary people.

These simple exchanges during the period of my early

grief were important in what became my search for what our Western culture does not teach us—a useful perspective on grief and its important role in our personal and communal development. Now years later, I see that my discomfort in answering the question, "How many children do you have?" was my own uncertainty, my grief illiteracy that caused me to doubt whether I could still claim that I have three children now that two of them have died. Could I still be their mother now that they have gone before me and become—what my friend from Malawi, Africa, Masankho Banda, taught me they are—my ancestors on the other side?

This led me to begin questioning how Western culture became so uncomfortable with grief. I knew that my experiences as a mourner did not always jive with what I had been taught as a social worker and practiced as a therapist. During the time of my university education and study of the great books, theories of grief were based on Freud, who, in his classic volume *Mourning and Melancholy*, recommended detachment from the deceased to move on with one's life. Current research supports the opposite, recommending that mourners find ways to continue a relationship with deceased loved ones, now referred to as "establishing and maintaining continuing bonds." So, misinformation hasn't helped.

In an op-ed for *The Washington Post* in February 2021, grief author Hope Edelman provided a brief history of grief. She pointed to two major cultural barriers that have caused Western cultures to get grief wrong: individualism and disconnection from the grief and mourning practices of ancestors. I would add a third- which is the adoption, across the globe, of the attitude of stoic reserve exhibited by the colonizers that created the British Empire, overriding the mourning practices of many of our ancestors who immigrated to this country.

I was an offspring of a "mixed marriage," an Irish-Catholic mother and a father who was a descendant of English and Northern Ireland Protestants. I observed a strong difference between the two sides of the family when, as a child, I was brought to funerals and wakes. Though both families came to America from the British Isles, one closely followed Victorian mourning practices, behaving in a reserved and stoic manner when a significant loss or death occurred. Keeping to the British stiff upper lip—the "keep calm and carry on" style of not letting emotions get the better of you—the relatives on my father's side were people of few words. Their physical presence was the support that was given. Upon hearing of the loss, they would drive through the night and into the early morning from their homes in rural Illinois to sit in near silence for hours on end in the front parlor of the deceased's family member's home.

In contrast, my Irish relatives did not subscribe to the notion that expressing one's feelings was a sign of weakness. Emotions abounded in their community gatherings, which were called "wakes." The atmosphere could be party-like at times, with whiskey and other alcoholic beverages being served. Members who never forgot they were once colonized by the British kept their own cultural traditions, expressing all manner of emotions. Some people might become argumentative, drunk, even disorderly—all behaviors accepted as expressions of their grief. A bereaved person that was especially close to the deceased might be put to bed and tended to throughout the night. Songs and stories were told and retold about the deceased's life, and others who had gone before them, leading to a celebration of the life of the deceased and the long arc of the family's survival. Highly prized would be a person who had what two Irish women I met in Brazil said of their Irish mother, "She's invited to lots

41

of funerals because she has the 'crack.'" When I asked them what they meant they said, "The wisecrack!"

Edelman also outlined how Americans' response to grief went from the "extravagant social affairs of Victorian mourning practices" of our great grandparents to treating "grieving as an individual affair, with mourners responsible for 'getting over their losses.'" Having so many deaths in such a short time, "the one-two punch of World War I and the 1918 influenza pandemic caused grief in America to go underground."

A century later, by the time of the Covid-19 pandemic, there was still no public memorial to the 675,000 people in the U.S. who lost their lives in that global event. Some say that the effort to "put it all behind and move on" left us ill prepared for the recent pandemic. Hopefully, if our culture becomes better at grieving this pandemic, we'll be better prepared for the next one.

The strong values people in Western culture hold of self-reliance, independence, and maintaining stoic reserve, though serving us well in some endeavors, have played a big part in our getting grief wrong. Author Mark Twain, who died a few years prior to the period Edelman referenced, wrote of his experience of the loss of his young daughter, Susy. He wrote to his minister of the "surcease of sorrow" that work provided him while acknowledging his ignorance of what the loss of his daughter would mean to his own life. "I did know that Susy was part of us; I did not know that she could go away; I did not know that she could go away, and take our lives with her, yet leave our dull bodies behind."

The architect Buckminster Fuller, who was born fifty years after Twain, proposed a concept that, though difficult to grasp in our individualistic culture, would have helped Twain understand his grief experience. "One is a fiction; the smallest indivisible unit is two people." Many cultures have simple expressions that keep before them an awareness of this interconnectedness of life.

"I am because you are" is a truth pronounced often in African and other communal cultures. In Korean culture, according to Presbyterian minister Mihee Kim-Kort, in her op-ed in *The New York Times*, "We are not separate from who loves us and whom we love." Her example is that people often don't call one another by their given names. Her mother and father would call one another "Mihee's father" and "Mihee's mother." Should one of their children die, they would not be surprised by the reaction Mark Twain experienced when he lost one of his children.

Sometimes children can get it right and demonstrate for us the fiction of our separateness and teach us what tears are for. My son Kenny was six years old when our family moved from Detroit, the town where the woman who had been his nanny for his whole life still lived. It was the hardest part of the move, especially for Kenny, and his teachers in Nebraska noted that he seemed to have some trouble engaging in the school's group activities. When he was with our family, he seemed fine, but at school, the teachers wondered if he might be depressed.

We arranged for Margaret to visit several months after we got settled in our new home in Lincoln, Nebraska. The visit lasted a week, and we all had a great time showing her our new surroundings. The day she left, I had an early morning meeting, so my husband and the kids took Margaret to the bus stop.

When I returned home in the evening, Kenny ran to greet me. He jumped into my arms and, somewhat breathlessly and with tears in his eyes, told me, "I've been crying and crying, and I can't stop crying."

"What are the tears saying?" I asked.

"They are saying, 'Margaret, Margaret, Margaret!'"

Ken continued to teach me functional ways to deal with emotions when he was diagnosed and lived with AIDS for four years. At that time, AIDS was a death sentence. He demonstrated much of what Brené Brown's significant work on emotions categorizes as "places we go when we're hurting." His *shock, overwhelm, and heartbreak* were palatable in the early months after his diagnosis, as was my need as his mother to resist the contagion of his emotions. Aware of my own strong emotions and the need to not inflict them on my son, I thought of myself as a warrior mother, needing to do what soldiers in the middle of battle must do—endure the pain without showing their own feelings, keep moving, and tend to what needs to be done. Fortunately, I had many supporters to allow me to express the *anguish* Brown identifies as the most intense emotion of early loss to prevent it from becoming a state of numbness, impacting the vitality of my present and future life.

Even though I knew the importance of expressing my sorrow, and I had the opportunity to do so at my women's spirituality retreats in east Texas, it took some encouragement for me to do it. During the time when my daughter was dealing with breast cancer, I was sitting close together in the women's circle with my friend Carol, struggling to keep it together, which of course meant stifling my tears. Moved by compassion, Carol caught on quickly to what I was doing. She placed her arms around me and whispered in my ear, "Mother's tears are sacred. Your tears are sacred." This landed in me as a novel yet intriguing notion. Perhaps it might not be necessary to apologize for losing my composure, for giving into my tears. Reaching across the room, Carol gestured to members of the group and said aloud, "Pass the sacred tissues." For the group, from that day forward, Sacred Tissues became the name of the tissue box that is always kept handy.

Artistic illustrations sometimes offer clarity regarding hard to define emotions. In her book, *Atlas of the Heart: Mapping Meaningful Connections and the Language of Human Experience*, Brené Brown offers a photo of a painting of a mother sheep standing over the murdered bodies of her offspring. The crows that presumably did the deed surround the scene. This painting in the National Gallery of Victoria in Melbourne, Australia has twice been voted the gallery's most popular work—once in 1906 and again more than 100 years later in 2011. The emotional theme of anguish after loss, for animals and people, is clearly timeless.

Even though we aren't supposed to talk about the pain and suffering in grief, we must talk about it. The cultural taboo against talking about our sorrows and other painful subjects inhibits our ability to fully recognize them, let alone grieve them. Losing someone or something central to our lives that we love is and will always be painful. Yet, support from others, or companioning, as it is called in the grief literature, reduces the pain, and helps us to bear it.

To be able to accompany someone who is grieving requires not just empathy but the ability to resist taking on the pain and suffering of the person as this is not helpful. When it happens, there are now two or more people in need of someone who can stay in a place of balance and calm, what Buddhists call *equanimity*. I learned this lesson while having lunch with my friend and former university supervisor Dr. Colleen Shannon. We had both learned of a dramatic loss in my career life. I had been turned down for tenure, despite having an 8-1 vote in my favor, after a six-year journey towards it.

Me: "I don't want you to hurt over this, because when I see you hurting, it hurts me double."

Colleen: "Oh, I will hurt because this is a hurtful situation. But I promise you, I will not suffer."

Me: "How are you going to manage that?"

Colleen: (Quoting an adage from Buddhism that I hadn't heard) "Pain is inevitable, suffering is optional."

Doing a bit of research, I learned that suffering comes from our attempts to avoid pain, and what we do to avoid pain often proves to only enhance it. This helps explain why the people who refuse to grieve or go near anyone who is grieving do not appear to be experiencing joy-filled happy lives. In our "there must be a pill for that" world, avoidance of pain becomes one of the most important barriers to grieving well.

Those who allow their feelings and who talk with others to process their losses—a therapist, a friend, or those who participate in support groups and community rituals, or who use the arts to grieve—come to appreciate what they've been through. They clarify the details of what happened and what part they played in it, and develop resources for their future lives. They are also able to stay centered and helpful when someone else is experiencing loss. Companioning involves connecting with others in such a way as to be able to take actions to help.

During the time I was being challenged by the illness and deaths of my best friend, my son, and later my daughter, I was a teacher and practitioner of InterPlay, an art-based system of improvisation, based in the body. Participants tended to be artists, therapists of various types, educators in schools, and ministers in church settings. We'd gather in workshop settings (or perhaps I should say playshop settings) to practice and witness one another using the dancing, singing, storytelling, and stillness forms of InterPlay to explore our lives and transform our sorrows and difficulties. Initially, we were a mostly white group with a few brave African American and Asian-American members. But as InterPlay spread to Australia, Malawi, Indonesia, and India, and we recruited more people of color to join us, they brought with them important concepts missing from our Western culture. Recognizing the art forms as practices used by their ancestors, and still in use today in many parts of the world, they named the art forms we were using "birthright practices."

Though we members of the dominant culture were not as familiar with the practices of our own ancestors as the African Americans and Indian Americans were, it wasn't hard to imagine that our ancestors processed their losses and supported one another through personal and large-scale communal changes by dancing, drumming, singing, storytelling, and other craft and art-making practices. Just as traveling to another country gives you a new perspective when you return home, the diversity of participants in our emerging communities helped us all to become more comfortable with our voices and bodies, and to experience the ancient and enduring ways that people throughout millenniums have processed their grief in community.

And then there is, in the water we swim in, the Western concept of time, which is not shared by indigenous and non-dominant cultures. The "get over it" message we hear regarding our grief is related to time as a commodity that is running out in our "hurry up" world view. We don't have time to remember the past or fully appreciate the present. When clients would get into that all too familiar place, I interrupted them by singing a few lines of a song popular in my youth. "Slow down, you move too fast. Gotta make the moment last... feeling groovy."

We have all absorbed many of the layered messages about grief and grieving that have surrounded us in our families, neighborhoods, schools, religious organizations, and the media. Some messages have been helpful, comforting when we've experienced disappointment and loss. I think of the ritual I learned as a child of lighting a candle for someone as a prayer for their healing. My understanding of the practice has changed, but it has continued to be helpful to me through the years in managing my own worries and sorrows and keeping me connected to those I love.

Other notions we've been taught are turning out turning out to be untrue about grief. Rather than the disconnection from what and who we have loved and lost, a better approach is to stay connected through ceremonies and practices of remembering as indigenous cultures have done and continue to do thorough out the ages. Cultures that honor and remember ancestors help people see themselves as connected to the web of life and its larger story. It helps to know that while individual people die, the love and the relationships they are connected to can continue throughout our lives, becoming a part of who we eventually become.

Artist Resource

Treat yourself and members of your family to the animated Pixar movie, *Inside Out*. You will learn about five emotions and the importance of feeling both positive and negative emotions.

Reflection/Action

The following questions are food for thought or exploration. You may choose to journal an answer to one or more of them.

1. When you were growing up, what were you taught about

emotional expression, particularly crying? How about anger?
2. Have you been in a situation where you felt it necessary to postpone feeling your feelings to take care of the business at hand? What did you do later to process your grief?

3. What is your go-to emotion when things don't work out as you would prefer?

4. What do you know about your ancestors and their ways of grieving losses?

Chapter Four

The Arts as Grief's Collaborator

"Would you like me to make a bracelet for you?" my nine-year-old granddaughter asks during our weekly session on Zoom. I say yes, partly because I know she's going to show me how she makes it, and our relationship now includes some time where she becomes my teacher. First, I must select the colors I want, and she shows the choices of the colors and charms that one must choose from. She tells me she made one for one of her best girl friends who is coming by this afternoon. "I would show it to you, but it's already wrapped up. She'll be surprised. It's part of a gift I'm giving her because her hamster died yesterday."

As she leads me through the design part of the process, she finally decides to open the gift package so I can see how one of the bracelets looks in its finished form. "You can put a word or name in the center if you have enough letters," she says, and I see that she has used the letter beads to create the word "hamster" on the bracelet. "I wrote a note, too," she adds, and I ask her to read it to me.

"I can be with you whenever you see this bracelet and think of me.

Signed, The Hamster."

It took me a while to process this exchange. I wasn't expecting that the note would be signed by the hamster, and that it would contain such wisdom about grief and the way art can serve the grieving process. I thought about how confused and uncertain we adults can be when we hear that a friend has lost a loved one—a relative, a beloved pet. What's the right thing to say? What can we do to offer comfort, to communicate that we care? I know there are still people who feel that children need to be sheltered from death and the processes of grieving. But Kyra is teaching me that perhaps we should be paying more attention to what young people may already know.

Seeing what Kyra has come up with for her friend confirms that empathy and creative imagination related to the art of grieving are possible at a fairly young age. Somehow, Kyra knows what to do, and I wonder how she learned it. She realizes that an art object can be a container in which to pour meaning. That it can provide encouragement, be a portal into beauty, and especially when given as a gift, be a reminder that the receiver is cherished and loved.

Perhaps it's because there is a place in the yard of her mother's house where pets are buried, and each of those burials was carried out in a somewhat elaborate, respectful ceremony. Perhaps it's because she was involved in assisting her mother in caring for her grandmother as Grandma Pat was coming to the end of her life. Perhaps it's because she and I sang songs together when the woman I always called my "sister grandmother" was terminally ill. We promised that we'd keep singing them after she was gone to always remember her. Perhaps it's because she was in the room of the small cottage when Grandma Pat crossed over into larger life several years ago, and reminders of Grandma Pat are sprinkled throughout many present-day conversations. Every now and then, someone, often Kyra's mother or Kyra, will say something and in the tone of their voice or the syntax of their message or in their gesture or facial expression, it will seem as though Grandma Pat has just entered the room. And perhaps it's like the hamster told Kyra's friend, "She's with us whenever we remember her."

What do we mean when we call something an art? The memorial bracelet Kyra created was certainly art in its own respect, and it's important that we keep our definition of art broad so that we don't limit the spectrum of self-expression. There is an official list of seven art forms, some dating back to when humans dwelled in caves, and others back to the ancient Greeks–painting, sculpture, literature, architecture, performance (theater and dance), and music. The newest art form, cinema, was added to the list in the 1920s when black and white silent films were created and eventually became moving pictures. Much is contained under many of those categories, but for the purposes of this book, art and art-making happen when a person uses skill, imagination, and creativity to express or communicate a message or bring into existence an object or arrangement of objects that demonstrate a sense of order and beauty. Common actions can be done with the kind of focus and concentration that they become an art in their execution and outcome. The art of cooking is not just getting the dinner on the table. It's cooking or baking with the kind of focus and intention that is used in any other kind of art-making. Some would say the cook puts in that secret ingredient of love, which is present in many practices of art-making.

Literature is a collection of written work which could be done in various styles, one of the simplest being writing letters to friends and loved ones. At times of great loss, this need may be especially compelling. Abigail Adams, when she learned of the death of a neighbor boy during the

Revolutionary War, wrote in a letter to her husband, "My bursting heart must find vent at my pen."

Writing in a journal is a time-honored personal and private way of processing life experiences, where we can note our joys and lament our sorrows. The practice often begins in childhood when an elementary school aged child is gifted a diary with a lock and key. This reassures the young author that siblings and parents will not be able to read what they have written. A question arises for elders who may have amassed a collection of journals throughout a long life. "Should I burn them before I die so there are no hurt feelings among my descendants?"

Essays on specific topics, prose, and fiction are included in this category, which reminds me of people I've known who, not wanting to keep their opinions to themselves, wrote letters to the editors of newspapers on political and social issues of concern.

The art of poetry is a literary art form that was lauded by the novelist Faulkner in his 1950 Nobel Prize acceptance speech. "The poet's voice needs not merely be the record of man, it can be one of the props, the pillars to help him endure and prevail."

Under the category of music, we need to mention playing an instrument or composing a tune, and collective activities like performing together in bands and orchestras. Singing can happen with others in a choir or chorus, on a group motor trip or alone in the shower. The music that is performed can be of rehearsed compositions or improvisational in the moment, structured like jazz. When music is performed for us, it can become a soundtrack for the activities of our lives, transporting us to the past, lifting our spirits in the present, and soothing our troubled souls.

Visual art is another way to categorize art forms. Often included in this grouping are painting, drawing, sculpture, collage, graphic design, photography, and architecture. According to neuroscientists, perceiving art is an aesthetic experience which stimulates the brain in areas associated with pleasure, memory, and emotion. Art-making in these visual art areas can take the maker into a state of flow, becoming one with the activity, as they follow their creative vision or intention. The artist becomes practiced at seeing information in a different light, putting unrelated items together, noticing patterns, and persisting through difficulties and failures.

The Performing Arts

I've always credited my mother for my involvement in the arts. She transmitted her love of dance to me by giving me what was denied to her, dance lessons beginning at age three. But standing back a bit in review of my life events, I have noted something very critical that fate and history provided as well when my father's company moved him, and our family, from the Chicago area to Louisville, Kentucky. It was the spring before my ninth birthday. By this time, I had already been studying dance for six years, even traveling alone on the elevated train from our home in Evanston to my classes in the city.

The story of the critical event that so affected my life began the year we moved to Louisville. As told to me, Charles Farsley, who served as mayor of the city from 1948 to 1953, discovered some unassigned funds left over from building a bridge across the Ohio River. The following year, he conceived what became the Louisville Fund for the Arts. He based its structure on that of the Community Chest, a nonprofit that raised money for social services, now known as Metro United Way. Starting with the seed money from the bridge, the fund raised $99,000 and funded The Louisville Orchestra, the Louisville Theatrical Association, Louisville Children's Theatre (now StageOne Family Theatre), and the Junior Art Gallery, the forerunner of the Louisville Visual Art Association. A couple of years later, the Louisville Civic Ballet was formed and included in the fund.

So, my siblings and I grew up in a city where the arts were considered as deserving and important as other community services. In this rich cultural environment, the focus was not just on art for children. My brother Miles did become involved in the children's theater, learning skills he used later in his career as a technical director and playwright. He and I took improvisational theater classes on Saturday mornings, enacting playful versions of the clamor and chaos that was our family life. We performed in productions of the Carriage House Players. We were the children in their production of Our Town and other shows, often as the only children in the cast. With our encouragement, our engineer father got involved in a production of a community theater group after we discovered evidence in a box in the basement of his thespian experiences at Purdue.

My sisters and I participated in the art classes at the library. My siblings and I played the three children of Fatima in a Catholic theater production, and during my years in high school, I danced in the ballet company and the opera. All the while, we played a part in raising money for the fund, walking the neighborhood with flyers and a small canister each year, enthusiastic ambassadors for the program, yet unaware at the time that no other city in the U.S. had such incredible resources.

In our capitalistic system, there can always be an

argument about whether a specific product of a creative process or the artist's skill meets the critical bar of excellence required of "fine or high art." This may be why many people hesitate to claim being an artist since that title seems reserved for a few highly cultured or exceptionally skilled people. According to some art critics, to be labeled art, the work must serve no practical purpose. It must exist for its own sake.

This is not what I mean when I refer to art that helps us to grieve. My interest is in art that is accessible to anyone and everyone, whether it is done on behalf of us—the observers, witnesses, or audience members—or when we engage in making the art ourselves. The benefit that can accrue to someone who uses an artform to assist them in grieving has no relationship to the grievers level of artistic skill or experience. In fact, an art that is unfamiliar to us can sometimes provide more wisdom and insight than one we may be more practiced in. Perhaps I should call the art I am referring to folk art—art that is from, by, and for just plain folks.

One category of art that is especially accessible comes under the heading of craft. This art in the service of practical creativity often results in useful handmade objects. Activities such as weaving, carving, pottery, embroidery, macrame, beading, sewing, knitting, quilting, glass blowing, and jewelry making transport the artist into a state of mind outside of ordinary consciousness—a place of flow and reverie.

Other creative activities considered necessary to maintain a household can be practiced as art, depending on the attention and intention of the practitioner¬. For example, the art of flower arranging, the art of gardening, the art of cooking, baking, home decorating. When these activities are done in a state of heightened awareness, one is not just getting dinner on the table or baking bread or weeding a flower bed. In a mindfully meditative space, ordinary actions become an embodied ritual, taking us into our intuitive mind—that part of us that Einstein called "a sacred gift," and that indigenous people call "the space between the worlds."

My best friend Rose was the first person I knew who had an inner clock on the grief spiral that brought her around each year to reflect again and again on the central loss of her life. Each fall season, around the anniversary of the tragedy of her mother's death in a house fire, I noticed my jovial, usually outgoing, community-organizing friend go to a place of inner reflection and appear sad and depressed. She'd begin rearranging furniture, organizing drawers and closets in her house, and she'd spend hours in the kitchen baking cookies and pies. After a week or so, she returned to her everyday life of involvement in the larger community and become, once again, the friend I knew.

Observing this yearly ritual, I didn't understand how these actions helped her honor her mother and facilitate her grieving, but I saw clearly that they did. We never talked about it, but now, from the perspective of a grief advocate who knows her backstory, it makes perfect sense. Rose was fifteen years old that fall day the school bus dropped her off a block or so from her house as usual. As she walked closer, she noticed flames coming out of the roof. She ran into the building and carried the badly scorched body of her younger sister out, saving her life. She was not able to save her mother's life because, as she learned later, the fire had started when a gas heater blew up in her face. Her mother died instantly.

In grieving loss, our rational mind is stymied. Grief is not a problem to be solved, a situation we can reason our way out of. Moving forward after the disruption of a significant loss requires us to enter our intuitive mind, yet life goes on and we must maintain ourselves in the material world. Anniversaries are about remembering.

In the grief spiral, the season automatically reminds

us, either consciously or unconsciously, of important loss events, so Rose is reminded. Her grief is for the loss of her mother, but also, she grieves and must accept again and again her inability to save her mother as she had saved her sister. Her creative actions of self and community care, of baking and arranging her home spaces, put her in a place of reverie, a place "between the worlds." I find it especially interesting that, though I never knew her mother, I'm sure they are actions that her mother would want her to take.

A main thesis of this book is that in grieving the inevitable and episodic losses in our lives, the arts can be profoundly helpful. This includes versions of all seven of the general forms of art listed and the sub-categories under them. "Art is the deliberate process of arranging elements in a way that appeals to the senses and the emotions," according to artist Marilina Maraviglia. And it is emotions and feelings that we must process and metabolize to make the life lessons inherent in grief available to us in our future lives.

Authors Susan Magsmen and Ivy Ross, in the introduction to their 2023 book *Your Brain on Art: How the Arts Transform Us* tell us that "we now have scientific proof that the arts are essential to our very survival... We've got the evidence on how the arts enhance our lives and build community." Referring to the arts as "the language of humanity," their book moves the reader beyond thinking of the arts as entertainment or escape, and documents through the new science of neuroaesthetics, or neuro arts, that the arts "alter our basic biology." For the audience and art-maker, they reveal, heal, and transform.

One of the biggest barriers for people to use any of the arts for their own betterment, whether to grieve losses, explore their body's wisdom, or connect in community, are the beliefs that "I can't sing," or, "I can't dance," or, "I'm not creative." When inviting students or clients into InterPlay, where we use many of these modalities to explore our stories, we often must convince people that what they are believing about themselves is not so. When teaching social work students, I begin by taking a poll in my classroom. "Raise your hand if you are someone who feels comfortable singing in a group." Perhaps half the students raise their hands, having had some experience singing in a church choir. "How many feel comfortable dancing in a group?" The number of raised hands for this question depends on the number of Caucasian men in the room, since due to cultural restrictions, they are unlikely to raise their hands. "How many of you would be willing to come up in front of the class and tell an impromptu story?" The response to this item might depend on how many social work students are currently working on a minor in theater. After the poll, I pose some final questions.

"Imagine all the students in this room are four years old, including you. Would you raise your hands to participate? How many other hands do you think would be raised when I ask, 'Who wants to dance? Who wants to sing? Who wants a turn at telling a story?'"

At this point, I describe to the group my image of what would happen if I asked these questions to a room full of four-year-olds. "This room would be full of enthusiastically raised hands, waving energetically, accompanied by shouts of, 'Pick me! Pick me! Pick me!'"

By adulthood we have lost something that once belonged to us. Few recognize what handicaps this inflicts on our ability to grieve and grow into the persons we were meant to be. Let's look at some of what we need when we are grieving and how the arts can help us address those needs.

I think of the arts as portals into our individual and collective creativity, igniting different intelligences. For my

60

friend and mentor Cynthia Winton-Henry, the co-founder of InterPlay, a form of collective creativity that uses a combination of various arts, the arts awaken soul wisdom, connecting us to our authentic selves. Susanne Langer, the twentieth-century art philosopher, in her book *Feeling and Form*, maintains that each art form accesses a realm of experience irreplaceable by any other art.

Early grief often begins and frequently cycles back to tiredness and fatigue. Shortly after my daughter died, I mentioned to an acupuncturist that I was having trouble eating. "I'm too tired to hold my fork," I told him. In a tone of recognition, he said, "Yes. Grief takes your chi, your life force." In this instance, following Langer's notion, if we want to engage a sense of energy and power, **dance** is the art form. Some of the after-loss fatigue is likely coming from all that we have been holding in our bodies before and during the loss. Releasing that while honoring our tiredness could look like a gentle stroll after a nap or a dance involving just one hand until one's energy begins to be restored. Then, it could be all-out, full-bodied movement since, as my dance teacher Harriet Berg expressed it, "Dancing doesn't take energy. It makes energy."

A major task of grieving is to accept the reality of our loss. To name it and claim it. But our brain will go in and out of this reality as it reconfigures itself—all those spiraling connections involved with our lost loved one or the dearly beloved situation have now become cul-de-sacs. The art of **storytelling** reminds us of what has been and of our life before this loss. Friends recall their experiences with our loved one and, like the way a prism splits white light into a rainbow, listening to their stories we come to know our loved one in a multifaceted, fuller way.

It's said that "grief is love with nowhere to go." After a significant loss, the griever becomes the one most in need

61

of love. Self-care and self-love are important actions to take during grieving, easier to take when we experience the love and support of others. The art form of **music** engages our sense of time, accompanying us through the pain, offering familiar and encouraging refrains. Beloved songs that have accompanied us at times of other losses reassure us that there will be a resolution to this episode of grief as well.

Since grief is not a solitary activity, the community, made up of those who companion us during our grief, offers support by coming together in the fullness of their **presence**. Since some stories are too big for one body to hold, the group body holds them with us, on our behalf. When the individuals and the group make space for our sense of overwhelm and fears about the future, it allows us to take space to process what we have been through. Neuroscientists have demonstrated that engaging in creating **visual art** helps us develop our sense of space and of ourselves in it. The act of creating something that has never existed before provides an antidote to our sense of loss and helps us adjust to an environment where an important someone or something is missing.

As a relationship ends, we need reassurance that the love on which it is based will never die. Viewing images of our loved one and of our life together created through the art of **photography** reinforces what will live on in memory throughout our lives. And following these enduring connections may mean changing our priorities to take actions to make the world a better place for our loved one having been in it, which demonstrates one of the gifts of grief—a renewed commitment to one's life purpose. The process, known as co-destiny, can inspire us to honor a loved one's life by taking actions that reinforce the values that they lived and that they did not live long enough to take.

The superpowers of the arts lie in their ability to transform individuals and communities from a less desired

62

state to a more ordered and peaceful one. Nowhere is this more clearly demonstrated than when various art forms are brought together in the rituals of a well-crafted funeral or memorial service. We enter heartbroken by our loss, and are soothed, unified, uplifted, and inspired by the beauty of the architecture and design of the space, the floral arrangements, the music, the laughter, and insights gained from the stories that honor the person's life, the poetry that is recited, the songs that are sung.

In our multicultural, pluralistic society, such harmony is not always easy to achieve. Members of different generations in a family often have different ideas about what customs to follow and how these rituals should take place. But in grieving our losses, there are universals.

"Art stops time," according to Bob Dylan. Now that life has turned out differently than we expected or desired, we long for closure. But in grief, there is no closure, unless we are talking about the person who has died. For those remaining, there can be a kind of resolution, a closure to an episode. Art, performed in the presence of witnesses, provides a way into our grief—a beginning, a middle progression, and a way out, an opportunity for completion of a particular chapter of our story in this time and place. As we leave the ritual space of chapel or gathering circle or burial ground, we are different than when we came in.

Though each life has specific losses and specific gifts of grace, we all share the common challenges chosen for us by history and fate. This is the raw material from which we fashion our lives. Like the artist who creates her art through the arrangement of found objects, we lead an artful life by making art out of what happens to us and discover that, in community with others on the path, order and beauty and repetitive musical rhythms are where our souls find their way home.

Artist Resource

Artists do more than just make art. Artists think systemically, contextually, and holistically. Artists synthesize complexity. Artists' processes are fundamentally about transformation and reorganization, destabilization, and reconfiguration.

The Grief Deck is a deck of flashcards that feature an image individually designed by an artist on one side, on the other, a suggested activity to do as you participate in *The Art of Grieving*. The cards in The Grief Deck inspire and invite people into an artistic process, taking what you know and applying it to a new frame, in this case, grief. The colorful images of hugs, flowers, water, and stones take us to the side of our brain where words are few but intuition and instinct live. The topics and suggested activities— "Helping Others Will Help Yourself," "Repetition and Healing," "Let Others Know What You Need,"—confirm that grieving is a verb, and provide wisdom on ways to move through its seasons of sometimes unanticipated yet continual change.

Artist Adriene Jenik and the organizations the Artists' Literacies Institute and the National Hospice Cooperative collaborated to produce this toolkit. Visiting the Artists' Literacies Institute website confirmed for me what my own experience and the experience of companioning others through their grieving process have taught. Grieving is an art, and one we can learn to do well. Using artistic processes, which are human processes, helps us "break through biases, old patterns of thought, and create, above all, knowledge and action."

Reflection/Action

1. What is your favorite art form to witness? What changes in you have you noticed when witnessing it?

2. Do you have a favorite art form to do? What effect does doing that art form have on you?

3. What barriers are you aware of that get in the way of you trying other art forms, either as a witness or a participant?

4. Have you ever been involved in the design of a funeral or memorial service? What arts have you found helpful in that effort? If not, do you have ideas about what you might choose in such a situation, either for a loved one's ceremony or for your own?

Part II
Application: Companioning

"We're all just walking each other home."

-Ram Dass

Chapter Five

Sweet Sorrow Through the Long Art of Grieving

Sorrow is an emotion more intense than sadness, and both are considered in many people's minds as something to get over, particularly in the years following a significant loss. But those who have traveled the long arc of sadness and sorrow through many revolutions of the grief spiral know that sorrow transforms through the years. It drops its connection to unhappiness and the wish for something else. Acceptance and gratitude for the love and life one has experienced become what I've come to call "sweet sorrow"—a resource in our present lives.

The Summer Solstice in 2017 was to be the twentieth anniversary of my son Kenneth's crossing. I searched for a way to honor him, especially on that day, and with a bit of inspiration from a Shakespearean quote and help from Interplay friends Christine and Jennifer and their SoulPrint Players improv troupe in Atlanta, I created a program called *When Parting Becomes Sweet Sorrow: Stories, Songs, and Celebrations of Those Forever in Our Hearts*. The presentation addressed the issues we face throughout the many years that we go on with our own lives after the loss of a precious loved one. In the invitational flyer, we posed some questions to consider:

- What reminds you of your deceased loved one? How do you respond?
- Do you still reference meaningful lessons learned from someone no longer with you?
- Have you found special ways to honor loved ones now deceased?
- Are you aware of ways you can extend the legacy of your loved one beyond their lifetime?

Profits from the event benefited an Atlanta agency serving people affected by HIV/AIDS. This was a way for me to practice co-destiny and extend the legacy of Ken's life beyond his own lifetime.

The purpose of the program was to explore lessons learned through the tough times, along with ways to live more fully in their aftermath. Using the dancing, singing, and storytelling forms of InterPlay, I told stories about Ken and called on troupe members to add their voices and stories of loved ones to mine. A slender young Black man jumped up from his seat in the audience and performed with the company, so I assumed he was a troupe member that I just hadn't met. Turns out, he came at the invitation of one of the members, and his skill and enthusiasm were contagious. In a talk back later with the audience, he engaged in an animated conversation, teasing me in his charming southern accent, "There you were, girl, up there on that stage, telling my story. How could you know my story? And Ken, it's like we're best friends." Later, I learn his name, Antron Reshaud Brown Olukayode, and that he was a dancer and performing artist living with AIDS, struggling as Ken did to take care of himself in that circumstance. I invited him to come to Pittsburgh to perform with my group, but he became ill and died of his disease before that could happen. I reached out to his mother, but she did not respond to my calls. I felt regret and sadness that we could not connect and share the common sorrow we had as mother's who have lost sons. I wanted her to know what Antron did for me and the memory of my son during the sweet sorrow event I had arranged in his honor.

What We Do with Our Pain

Most every loss is painful, and often in its immediate aftermath, excruciatingly so. For the newly bereaved, the pain might not be experienced as sorrow, let alone sweet sorrow. Our bodies and minds, and our culture, offer up a smorgasbord of possible emotions: shock, denial, anger, fear, depression, and despair, but sadness and sorrow are not even on the often-repeated stairstep list of grief responses. Holding on to our reactions to loss in our bodies, we risk dulling our own senses and experiencing a diminishment of vitality in our own lives. We have little sense that the pain will take us anywhere, so we search for anything that will distract or diminish its intensity. But this failure to process our pain, to grieve our losses, means that we risk inflicting that pain on others, as hurting people often hurt other people. In failing to grieve our losses, we are disconnected from others on life's journey with us, so isolation and loneliness engulf.

In looking at the profiles of some of the young people who have committed horrendous acts of mass murder, they often had grievances (grief) around being rejected, mistreated, or overlooked. I wonder what could happen if teachers or other community members recognized and reached out to help the person address their pain and process it in a healthy way.

Getting to the blessing of sweet sorrow takes years of turnings on the grief spiral, the faithful processing of loss, the practicing of grieving as an art, and coming together in ritual and ceremony to exchange stories that honor the lives of deceased loved ones. Through these processes, our sorrow matures, as fine wine matures, into sweet sorrow, where the blessings in the losses can be fully appreciated and celebrated.

After a Long Life Together

Losing a loved one at the end of a long life, we get to review all the chapters of the story and see how the story and our part in it turned out. The weekend after my seventy-nine-year-old sister died, I was flooded with memories of her and the long life we shared together. It's amazing how present she has become now that she has made her transition. Pat slept in the twin bed next to me most every night for the first eighteen years of my life, and the first fifteen years of hers. Too often, according to our father, we'd keep one another awake past our bedtime. "Quiet down up there, you girls," he'd yell up from the living room below. In response, we'd lower our voices to the barest whisper but continue our conversation in the dark. After a while, in our enthusiasm, our voices would rise again, provoking another warning from our increasingly frustrated father. Sometimes we'd get loud enough to wake our younger sister, Mary Jane, who slept in a youth bed across the room.

There's a part of this story I've never told to anyone outside the family, but we've recounted it to one another often at family gatherings throughout the years. It was the time that our father's reaction to our continued talking exploded with impatience and anger and, unable to restrain himself, he stormed up the stairs and began to physically accost Mary

Jane, whose bed was nearest the door. Pat and I knew we were next, and that we were solely responsible for getting our father to this state of frustration, so we jumped out of our beds and tried to restrain him, all the while shouting, "Dad! She was asleep! She didn't have anything to do with this."

Ever afterward, Mary Jane, who was four or five years old at the time she was awakened out of a sound sleep in this horrific manner, always maintained, laughingly, that this was why she turned out to be such a weird person. Talk about a functional reframe of a past trauma! I appreciate now that how we tell and retell the story, with support from others in the story, can heal it.

I suspect Pat and I began our adventurous journeys together earlier than most kids. At ages seven and four years old, our parents put us on a train in Chicago to travel alone to Detroit, Michigan. We were met by Auntie and Aunt Dote, my mother's sister and aunt. A favorite image from that daylong train ride is of a blonde curly-headed Patty Jo, standing at the train's water fountain, despite my many admonitions, filling yet another white cone shaped paper cup with cool water to bring back to her seat. Fortunately, she didn't have to travel far since we sat very near that awesome water fountain.

After we each graduated high school, we went our separate ways. I went to New York to dance, and Pat stayed in Louisville, working for the American Telephone and Telegraph Company—a first job for many young southern women high school graduates of that era. One of the stories that still survives in my memory was Pat's response to the racist practices of her employers. The telephone company sales representatives, whose job it was to sell princess phones (one for each room of the customer's house, if possible), were told to mark an "A" for "African" on the record of Negro customers so they could be easily identified. "I just marked

73

an 'A' on every card to stand for 'American,'" Pat told me a few months before she quit to find a job more compatible with her own value system.

Instead of college, Pat joined The Grail, a Catholic women's lay organization, which at the time had 14,000 women participating in programs in twelve city centers around the country. She studied and lived at their center in Loveland, Ohio, near Cincinnati, working in the bakery and learning from the older Grail members who were pioneers in Catholic feminist theology. Women in the arts, and the ecumenical and civil rights movements of the time. Pat was sent to a migrant camp in northern Michigan where she organized and directed a school for the children who missed a great deal of school as they traveled and labored beside their parents. This led to her involvement in the Cursillos Movement, and her recruiting me to join her in leading weekend retreats for women, most of whom were twice our age.

We don't have a word for the loss of a sibling. Orphans are people whose parents are deceased. Widows have buried their husbands, widowers their wives. But the death of a sibling is often overlooked, or its importance minimized. Pat and I, like other siblings, were each other's first best friend. We shared experiences and memories that lasted a lifetime. Yet, my sister's memories didn't last her entire lifetime. Driving away from the Gerontology Center in Ann Arbor after some testing a few years ago, I remember her frail sounding small voice coming from the back seat of the car, "If I have what they say I have, I could lose myself."

As her disease progressed and her memory faded, she did lose herself, but since I was there for so much of her life, I found a way to give some of it back to her. Visiting in person, and later, on an iPad held by a gracious and generous healthcare worker, I would reminisce about things we'd done together. She'd smile and her eyes would sparkle like she was remembering and reliving it with me. Or maybe she was enjoying it all for, what seemed to her, the first time.

Pat's life ended early Saturday morning August 21, 2021, in the ICU of a hospital in Boston. She had been sent there with a medical emergency by the facility where she had lived bedridden with late-stage dementia for several years. The hospital called me Friday morning as they were unable to reach her son. "The medical record says to do everything we would do for a thirty-year-old, and I don't think that's appropriate," the heart specialist said. I agreed and pleaded with him to avoid taking dramatic measures until her son, who was the official guardian, landed at an airport and was able to communicate her wishes. Once we got ahold of my nephew, Adam, both the doctors and I urged him to continue to Hawaii for his all-expense paid vacation with his wife. The doctors were sure there was nothing he could do for his mother if he returned, and I was sure if she knew the situation my sister would say, "Don't you dare come back here and give up that trip you won from your employer." With phone calls back and forth and kind and caring physician residents, we were able to reduce Pat's suffering and secure for her a peaceful transition after this way-too-long disease and it's way-too-long goodbye.

Unexpected Grief After a Long Separation

Another experience of loss and grief that is not written about often or understood, even for those going through it, is that of a former spouse. In my case when my former spouse, George, became gravely ill, we had been divorced for nearly half a century.

I awoke feeling shaky one Friday morning. It took me a while to translate the meaning of that bodily signal and its relationship to my state of wellbeing. Staying with it during a morning meditation, the sensation developed into a subtle sadness. After a few more moments, I remembered that the night before, a couple of hours before going to sleep, I had received some not good news regarding George. In a text from my son-in-law Bill, who was in Oregon checking on him, Bill wrote, "He has hit a rough patch... He's fallen a number of times. He's weak, sleeping all the time, and not really eating. A suggestion was made that a hospice evaluation be done..."

The body remembers, and more than just what happened the night before. George and I were married sixty-one years ago, longer than many of my students and younger friends have been alive. I have been divorced from this man for forty-seven years. We co-parented three children together and buried two of them. I've been married to my present husband, Richard, for forty-three years, many of those years spent co-parenting with George, whom Richard laughingly referred to as his "husband-in-law."

In allowing this sadness, my body teaches me more about the process of grieving—a process I know to be episodic, lifelong, and necessary to metabolize loss. But more than a decade and a half-century ago? Isn't it time to be over it? Or through it? But grieving one loss often opens opportunities to grieve some prior losses hiding underneath or behind it.

Throughout the weekend, as the group text updates on George's condition continued, I feel in touch again with those promises: "in sickness and in health, till death..." I'm in touch again with the courageous, trusting twenty-two-year-old bride who made those promises. She is letting me know now that she's still heartbroken that she couldn't keep them.

The following morning, when I was online with my

woman's group, I checked in with them saying that though the patriarchy might say I spent the morning "feeling sorry for myself," I will say that I've spent the morning "having my sorrow," well-earned and well-deserved. The group responded by taking a few moments to raise their hands to the screen and create an energetic grid, sending me love and support in the silence, with instructions to send it on to family members who may need it. This helped me identify another loss I'm grieving. This one is connected to a family member I would like to support during this episode with George, but our estrangement makes that impossible. I'm soothed to realize that I can still offer prayers and good wishes for George, and for everyone touched by George's life.

In the spiral dance of grief, as we come around again to anniversaries, birthdays, rites of passage, and deaths, we miss again those gone from our sight. These cyclical occasions can be opportunities to connect again with our loved ones, and with who we were when they were here with us. When I was raising my three children, especially during the time I was a single mom, my definition of a friend was someone who helped me be a good mother to my children. Now that I've buried two children, a friend is someone who helps me remember them.

My friend Pam and I each have a son who died young. Neither of us have met the other's son, but we try to make a point of marking our sons' birthdays or death days by sending a card or sharing lunch or a walk in the forest. Our sadness softens into "sweet sorrow" as we companion one another, focusing on the gift our sons' lives have been to our lives. And we each get to know someone we've never met in person.

My grandson Ethan has a modern technological version of sharing the sweet sorrow of his mother Corinne's life and loss with his friends through his Facebook account. In 2020, when we were all struggling with the Covid-19 shutdowns, he posted an excerpt of something she wrote during her struggles with failing breast cancer treatments: "There are times I have looked back at the last nine months of disappointments. Being through a fire refines us to beautiful gold, but first we must be hot to achieve this. The heat of the fire is NOT comfortable as we stand in it. But I look forward to getting out of the fire, standing back from it, and enjoying its warmth and beauty."

Ethan posted this reply: "She is enjoying that beauty now next to her Lord and Savior Jesus Christ. But we still walk in that fire. This year the flames are burning hotter than ever. If you find yourself burning, inhaling too much smoke, wondering when we can get out of this 2020 fire, keep the faith! One day, God willing, we'll be out of this fire, appreciating the lessons we learned from it. I love you Mommy, thank you for continuing to inspire us today!"

Ethan's social media post demonstrates two of the central gifts of grieving well: the wisdom that keeps coming through the years as we look back and reflect with new eyes, and the compassionate heart to be there for others. As Ethan is still learning from his mom, and as we all continue learning from him, he reinforces what I teach others and try to remember to do myself. Here's his P.S.: "If you're struggling through this time, don't suffer alone. Reach out to someone you trust and allow others to help you carry your burdens... That's something I learned from my mother. I'm happy to be that person for you, just reach out and let's talk!"

Connections with the Past

Many cultures have time-honored traditions that encourage people to establish and maintain enduring connections with

78

deceased loved ones throughout their lifetimes. African American women friends have shown me the way many in their culture follow the West African notion of *Sankofa*. The word in the Twi language of Ghana means "to retrieve," and it's represented by the image of a mythical bird whose feet are planted facing forward while its head is turned backwards. The bird is carrying a precious egg in its mouth, representing the future and the notion that we must go back in order to go forward. This perspective allows us to connect with the dreams that those who came before us had for themselves and for us.

When we decorate walls or mantles in our homes with images of loved ones, visit grave sites, or on special occasions cook recipes and serve the food in dishes handed down from ancestors, when we wear jewelry or clothing gifted to us by loved ones, we are retrieving the loving connections that cause us to be able to say, "I am because they were."

During the long arc of grieving, sometimes our own homes hold surprising messages from the past. When my husband was setting up his home office during our sheltering and working from home phase a few years ago, it was necessary to move a large cabinet that had been in our second-floor guest room for over a dozen years. Removing all the books it held created a major mess but also the opportunity to sort and cull our book collection. Before placing the books on the shelves of our new bookcase, I asked two questions: "When did we get this book?" and "Will we ever look at it again?"

That's when it started to happen. I noticed occasionally that a book turned out to contain a forgotten treasure. *Living with a Life-Threatening Illness* almost made the gifting pile until I noticed an envelope inside. It was a holiday card from our youngest son Kenneth. He had added a personal note to the text. "Thanks for your support, from your son and friend,

Kenneth." I don't know if he gave us the book or whether I put the card inside later because the note's message was so connected to the book's theme. The date on the card was December 1993—the month and year Kenneth was diagnosed with AIDS.

Though it was a task I had dreaded, after this first precious "voice from the past," I progressed through my book-sorting task with a grateful heart and the sweet sorrow of precious memories coming to life. My next discovery was in *The Book of Qualities* by J. Ruth Gendler, a slender volume I remember receiving as a gift from my best friend Rose. What I'd forgotten was the letter from her inside its pages. It was dated Nov. 11, without the year. Rose mentions the election, and she died in the fall of 1995, so 1992 had to be the date. Her note is congratulating us on putting an offer in on a beachfront condo she and I discovered on one of our visits to Corpus Christi, Texas. "It will be great to have a place to go to, at least 14 days a year," she teased, referring to the regulations on how often you can personally use an investment property.

After these two discoveries, I slowed down to look inside each book, to be sure I wasn't missing a significant dedication or insert. When I came across *The Women's Encyclopedia of Myths and Secrets* by Barbara G. Walker, I was rewarded doubly. The front piece contained two hand-written notes dated September 5, 1987, the date we opened our behavioral health care clinic, *Iatreia Institute for the Healing Arts.* Our friend and clinic manager Jyoti King had written: "To Sheila – To remind her of the Power-Here's to the Victory of Transformation, Love, Jyoti." Her husband, our business advisor and friend, wrote: "To Sheila, On this day of passage, a reminder of those who have traveled this way before. You are not alone. You are not the same. Love, Randall."

Now that I've discovered the bookcase as a place of

hidden treasures, of messages from those who have gone from our sight, I wonder what will happen in the future as we rely more on digital versions of our books.

Lessons From a Photograph

I came across a photo I took last fall while hiking in the Laurel Highlands in Pennsylvania. Looking at it now, I feel again the chilling breeze, the dangerously slippery wet leaves underfoot, the disappointment that the fall colors we expected to see in the high canopy had been scattered by the winds before we arrived and settled on the ground below.

We didn't expect to have to look down to admire the various colors now strewn on top of and in between blue slate rocks. I was further disappointed that my plan to collect some leaves to bring home had been made impossible by recent drenching rains.

Now spring in Pennsylvania disappoints again with cold and rainy weather. As the resident caretaker to our community garden's plants, I brought in what could be brought in recently, and covered the rest as recommended by the local weatherman. Frost was intended for pumpkins, not vegetables and flowers just emerging in spring.

A reminder of a treacherous trail, my photo illuminates for me a truth I was not aware of when I took it. Everything dies, in its appointed time or beforehand. My photo helps me see again the intricacies of the decay, the beauty in the decline—a symbol of the long arc of grief and its many faces in the changing seasons.

Grieving War and Its Atrocities

Practicing the art of grieving throughout the years and using the arts to do that has continually offered me lessons and learnings not available through any other method. I've lived through many armed conflicts and declarations of war, some involving my own country and other countries far from our shores. When Israel was attacked by Hamas-led Palestinian militant groups and declared war on them in the fall of 2023, what followed for me were deep lessons in the need for communal grieving and how to do it.

I was out of the country, off the grid so to speak, when war came. It was alerted by a text from a student who lives in Israel and who regularly attends my online Friday morning class. I knew that David and his wife had moved to Israel from Pittsburgh relatively recently to be close to children and grandchildren, so I thought that many members of his family could be at risk. On my trip home, through airport lounges and while seated on several planes, I closed my eyes often and sent compassion and peace to David and his family and all those living in harm's way.

On the following Friday during our Zoom class, David's face on the screen brought instant joy and relief to me and the members of the class who were from various parts of the US. He described how he had first learned about the conflict when he was at the synagogue. Everyone was sent home to shelter in the sealed off rooms that most apartments and homes in Tel Aviv have, so he and his family were feeling safe at that point. When we played our "I could talk about …" game, David mentioned he could talk about how good it felt to be greeted with "soft tones and smiles" when he came online, and he could also talk about his "deep desire for ease." He couldn't stay until the end of class, but the group decided to finish our time together by dancing on his behalf, which is the InterPlay form we consider a prayer.

Looking up at the list of songs on my playlist to select one to accompany our dancing for this occasion, the song "Kinder" by the acapella singing group *Copper Wimmin* caught my eye. I was especially drawn to the album's title, which I had never noticed before: *The Right to Be Here*. A strong kinesthetic signal in my body confirmed the irony in using this song for this occasion. Wars and armed conflicts are, at their core, a fight over who has a right to live in a particular place or who has the right to live at all.

As the other participants and I followed and led one another through the dance, the song took me to a place that its lyrics suggested. In the face of horrific war, injustice, fear, and death, "I decided to be happy, I decided to be glad, I decided to be grateful, for all I ever had." We felt those sentiments and sent them to David, remembering what he desires is "smiles and soft tones."

Later that afternoon, I realized how good I had been feeling since the morning visit with David and dancing on his behalf. I began feeling something that grievers often feel, a kind of guilt that we are allowing ourselves to feel good when the loss we are grieving, or that those around us are grieving, is so great. I questioned whether feeling good was the right response to the difficult situations that people I know and people I don't know are being faced with around the globe.

Just then, a notice came into my email box to join a *Community Vigil for Our Collective Pain,* sponsored by one of my favorite organizations, Reimagine. Their mission is to host programs that reimagine loss and channel life's challenges into meaning and growth. I know vigils to be a time of keeping awake, of coming together in silence with others after something horrific has occurred, to slow our responses down to enable clear attention and awareness, to offer prayers for those affected, including ourselves. This opportunity seemed just the right one for me on this occasion.

I joined 146 other people online as the organizers made clear about what kind of space this was to be: "to unite in sorrow as our compass points towards mourning loss and widening our hearts with love." The organizers were clear also about what kind of space it was not¬¬. It was not "a blaming space, a religious space, a political space, or a solution space." While the complexities of this world-shaking event include elements of all of that, we were intent on uniting and grieving our collective pain.

Musician Phoenix Song greeted us by playing the flute as a visual of a flower-adorned altar was interspersed with her image and instrument on our screens. The director outlined the ceremony and invited us to light a candle in the spaces where we were coming in from around the world. Several participants repeated the line, "In lighting our candles, we mourn division, terrorism, violence, war, trauma, hatred, and all that is disconnected from love."

Phoenix Song led us in a meditation ceremony involving chanting, three ahs for ourselves, three ahs for one another, and three for the world and those affected by the conflict beyond our screens. We repeated chanting these ahs to send loving kindness, then compassion, then joy, then ease, and then equanimity.

When we extinguished our candles, several people repeated the line, "We release light into our world to keep alive hope and the memories of those we honor, today, tomorrow and for the rest of our lives."

The session ended in breakout rooms, and I was partnered with a man from Australia. He mentioned that news of this war was coming to his family as they are in mourning for his wife's sister who had killed herself a few weeks earlier.

I expressed my condolences to him and his family, realizing again that personal and family losses continue to occur and overlap with the larger societal ones.

That evening, I played the song again for myself and moved to it to reinforce those decisions that the song had caused me to make: "I decided to be happy, I decided to be glad, I decided to be grateful, for all I ever had." Instead of asking myself, "How can you be happy when so many in this world are suffering," the question changed to "How can you **not** keep present to what everyone in the conflict is hoping for, for themselves, their families, their communities, and for the world?" Could it be **the obligation** of those of us not living in the center of the storm to keep alive the loving, peaceful energy that the world will need to get us all there?

Artist Resource

Check out LetsReimagine.org. New events, most of them online, that explore, grief, loss, and self and community care are added regularly.

Visit the Liberty Legacy Memorial website and learn more about the Sankofa bird and how the art symbol communicates how the past can serve as enrichment for the present and a guide for the future.

Reflection/Action

1. Look around your living space and see if you can identify items given to you by deceased loved ones. Select one such benefactor to write a thank you letter to for gifts of habit or knowledge that you received from them. Let them know how

this gift has played out in your own life.

2. Hope Edelman, Author of the book *The After Grief: Finding Your Way Along the Long Arc of Loss,* believes "our stories of loss remain in transition, steadily evolving as we continue to learn, mature, investigate, and experience." Choose a particular loss of a loved one from long ago and write about it now from the perspective of the insights and experiences you have had since then. Edelman uses the image of standing in the center of a giant infinity sign, casting back into memories of the past and bringing them forward into projections of our future. Note how different this version of the story is after many revolutions of the grief spiral from the one you would have written or told more immediately to when it happened.

Chapter Six

Illness, Aging, Disabilities, and Diminishments: Good Will Come from This

You know the popular phrase. "What doesn't kill you makes you stronger." But that message isn't entirely accurate. We become stronger (or not) depending on how we react to a challenge. We're all familiar with athletes and adventurers who give themselves death-defying challenges: rock climbing, skydiving, bungee jumping—danger-filled adventures where a person could die. But what about the millions of people who face death-defying challenges not of their own choosing, like dealing with a life-threatening diagnosis like cancer, or a debilitating injury that threatens what's possible in one's future life? Everyone knows someone, you may be that someone, who has received such a diagnosis or limiting prognosis after an accident. These challenges of grief and loss involve letting go of what we had in mind for our lives, or at least a particular period of it. How we grieve these challenges to our health and wellbeing, how we respond, determines who we become.

The impact of these challenges falls not only on the person who receives them but on the people in their family and social support network whose lives are changed as well. Being one of the eight people that research tells us are likely to be connected to someone diagnosed with an illness or facing a limited prognosis is how I came to *The Art of Grieving*. I joined the club that none of us ever wants to belong to when my best friend was diagnosed with breast cancer, followed soon after by my son's diagnosis of AIDS in 1993. Disease and disability don't just happen to the person the doctor diagnoses in his or her office. It happens to the whole family, and often the surrounding community, igniting a anticipatory grief and fear for a loved one's life, and for the end of life as we have known it. The journey is often treacherous, if not terrifying, and often includes some elements of a taboo, a stigma, or even shunning.

My mother had died of pancreatic cancer ten years before. While she and my father, who was her caregiver during her sickness, searched for a diagnosis, I lived in another state, not fully aware of her suffering. I made a visit to humid Louisville, Kentucky the late summer before she died. While Dad was attempting to install a window air conditioner, my mother and I were sitting in the backyard, attempting to cool off. Running water from the garden hose over our legs and feet, I noticed how thin Mother had become, and that it hadn't affected her lovely shapely legs. I asked her, "What do you think is wrong with you?" She shook her head and said in a soft voice, "I didn't know."

My father told me a neighbor recently took him aside and said, "I'm so sorry to see your wife has cancer." His comment likely related to how emaciated she looked. The doctors couldn't confirm any diagnosis, and in fact, during the medical appointment I witnessed, they behaved as though they didn't believe my mother's pain was real. As she sat silent and sullen on the table, a doctor said, in an aside to my father,

"We may be dealing with a touch of Alzheimer's here."

I felt my mother's anger rise in her, and mine rise in me. Neither of us spoke, but I wanted to say, "Mother is not hard of hearing, and she is a nurse. The anger you see in her flashing eyes is not due to mental disability or disease. It is because she understands you don't believe her." Her cancer diagnosis was confirmed only a few days before she died. Later, the autopsy confirmed there was no sign of "a *touch* of Alzheimer's."

Having symptoms without the confirmation of a diagnosis or a treatment plan was, in addition to the physical pain, a lonely road of angry angst and self-doubt. Aside from her sister's frequent visits and Dad's support, she experienced her grief without the support and companioning of family and community.

Illness and injury are experiences of loss and limitations, resplendent with lessons to be learned. One of my earliest experiences of this was when my nurse mother took me to meet a patient who had been treated in the hospital where she worked. It was clear that my mother admired Carolyn. She spoke of her in awe and amazement as to how she lived the life of a "shut in" that fate had assigned her. I don't know what was wrong with her, but her sickness was not something that the doctors could make better.

I must have been four years old when we first visited this frail young woman in the facility where she lived. I had to look up at her through the bars that surrounded the bed she was lying in. To me, it was like a cage, like the youth crib that my toddler brother slept in. It was strange to see a grown woman in that kind of a bed. Because my mother said she was, "bedridden" I decided the bars were to make sure she didn't fall out. Her whole life was lived in that bed. No sitting up in a chair, no going outside for walks. She couldn't even visit anyone. She had to wait for people to visit her.

My mother and other people did visit her. They reported she was always in a good mood, never complaining, offering up her discomfort, accepting her situation as God's will. We would bring prayer requests to her to pray for us because that was what she would do with her time. She was like a saint who was closer to God than other people.

Fast forward a half century or more and my daughter Corinne is in a hospital in Houston having a bone marrow transplant. One wall of her room is a gallery of photographs of people, friends, relatives, some total strangers. Before she decided on the bone-marrow transplant, she made many trips to Houston from her home in Lincoln, Nebraska, participating in drug trials to find one that would address her particular type of breast cancer. A drug would initially work and then it would stop working, and they would try another one.

This was before social media and a friend suggested that rather than having to spend time on the phone once she got home, updating people on the rollercoaster ride we were on, she could write an email on her way home. Susan would then distribute it to Corinne's email list. These emails became a kind of journal of the gifts she received from strangers, such as the hotel room donated by a son of one of her friends. There were stories of the special friendship she had with her regular taxicab driver, Emanuel, whose whole church were praying for her. These letters became so interesting and inspiring that people forwarded them to friends and family who didn't know Corinne.

Once a bone marrow transplant was proposed by her physicians and it was determined that no blood relative was a good enough match, the people on the list became involved in the quest to help her find one. In the space of a couple of months, an unusual ten-point match—an unrelated fifty-one-year-old male donor—was found. Corinne took this as a sign that it was God's Will and decided on the procedure. When she learned that she would be in a hospital room for two weeks in isolation, she said, "What am I gonna do with myself? I'm not gonna be feeling that sick, and I don't want to be just nervously focusing on myself." She got the idea of praying for the people who had been praying for her and she asked them to send her their pictures. By the time of her discharge to the apartment we were to live in for the next three months, the mail had brought enough photos to fill two gigantic poster frames that I used to transport them in. Corinne continued praying for these people, and more who were added as she received the infusions to prevent Graft vs. Host disease—a situation where her system rejects the new immune system, or the new immune system attacks her.

Though I had never spoken about my experience with Carolyn, Corinne's prayer wall reminded me of her, and now years later, I see Corinne and Carolyn's acts as examples of a reaction to a challenge that strengthens the person responding to it. Their radical acts of love are what the Christian tradition calls *redemptive suffering*. The persons performing such actions are themselves transformed by them.

Living with Limitations

Mitch was a s math professor, musician, and Shakespearean actor when he contacted me. He had discovered an interview I had done a few years before on the public television station in his state of Georgia. He was convinced that I was the person he should work with to deal with his grief in response to the overwhelming number of losses he had experienced in recent years.

The initial loss had been the diagnosis of Parkinson's Disease, a chronic movement disorder he would be living with the rest of his life. Mitch's diagnosis, at the age of 53, was classified as "early onset". Shortly thereafter, Mitch went through a divorce. His children moved away to go on with their own lives. Fortunately, he was able to renew his relationship with his high-school sweetheart. However, when the pandemic hit, his girlfriend succumbed. At the time of our phone call, he was recovering from a bone marrow transplant he had undergone for a blood disease.

In my life, at the time of Mitch's call, I was confined to my dance studio turned media studio due to the pandemic, working on a book proposal for *The Art of Grieving*. As a dancer, I had heard about programs that dance companies were offering for Parkinson's patients, so maybe I could help. For sure, I would learn a lot, which are the two criteria I use for taking on a client.

It was a good match. Aside from the trouble I had tracking his description of a revolutionary math equation he was working on, his music compositions and his continued participation in an online theatre group connected with what I was trying to write about: how the arts can help us grieve and live our best lives.

I learned a lot about the horrific disease he was living with as he dealt with the annoying symptoms of stiff muscles, restlessness, sleep disorders, and a sometimes slow shuffling gait. But it was the debilitating immobility or "freezing" that could come on, unannounced at any moment, day or night, that most impacted his ability to live his life as he would want without assistance. As we worked together to help him use his creative intelligence and artistic skills to manage a life that provided the most dramatic of challenges, Mitch's life confirmed a saying of Moshe Feldenkrais, the Israeli engineer and somatic educator that I quote often, "The quality of your life is the quality of your movement."

Frequent incidents of profound helplessness could bring a halt to any endeavor, from crossing a room to a trip to the neighborhood pharmacy. Attempting to do the simplest things required heroic measures, and I was awed by how he continued to reach out to neighbors, family members, old friends, and to bravely make new ones online. He continued to research and try out new treatment approaches, and we explored creative ways to combat the anxiety and depression that sprang from the limitations the disease placed upon him.

Mitch composed musical pieces and shared some with me to use online as warm-ups while teaching InterPlay. I teased that it was like I had commissioned the music specifically for the purpose of the warm-ups because of the way they fit so well into the choreography. But part of the purpose his music served was to keep his own spirits lifted.

Mitch often asked out loud the questions anyone dealing with the pain and devastation caused by serious illness and the attempts to treat it have. Is this version of life, under these circumstances, a life worth living? If not, what can I do to make it worth living? What am I willing to do to make my life better? And how can I go on?

With many illnesses and diseases, patients accept a painful treatment regimen that strongly impacts the quality of their present life in the hope that they can return to some semblance of what could be considered a normal life. But, when the treatment doesn't cure or cause remission, or when the disease returns after remission, the questions return. Is it time to let nature take its course? Is it time to discontinue treatment, get your affairs in order, and enjoy whatever time you have left?

Physician and author, Bernie Siegel's words ring true

here. "When the future is uncertain, there is nothing wrong with hope." That's one of the lessons a serious illness can teach us. In January of 1993, my son Ken was recuperating at my home after a hospital stay where he had been treated for pneumonia. He developed a rash and, despite being admonished by his father and stepfather that I should not "over-react," I took him back to the hospital to get it checked out. The emergency room doctor located his chart and, in the presence of my son and I, began reading it out loud, "Twenty-eight-year-old male, HIV status – positive." He paused, looked at us over his glasses and said, "You didn't know? No one called you?"

My reaction? I looked into the eyes of my terrified son and decided I needed to be strong. I needed to be a warrior mother. Since I felt very far away from that reality, I said a silent prayer for myself that I'd be able to fake it till I made that needed strength my reality. After a few weeks, my son's reaction was a more helpful one. "Okay. I have AIDS, but I don't have to accept that I'll die of it. I believe that the cure for AIDS is right around the corner so it's my job to take radical care of myself so I will be here for that day." This attitude sustained him, and me, throughout the ups and downs of the four years he lived with the disease.

Injury

Injuries are about as common and likely as loss. The disabilities they create are often temporary, but grief and loss come in the aftermath, and sometimes we don't even have to do anything unusual to sustain an injury. My dancing social worker friend, Lynn, stepped off the sidewalk and onto the curb one evening when coming out of a restaurant and broke her ankle, putting her on crutches and in a boot for months. Subscribing to the "the show must go on" principle, she kept on traveling to her day job at the university, but she couldn't drive, and had to get help with transportation and carrying her heavy school bag back and forth to her home.

Dancers and athletes navigate injuries as occupational hazards. When I was in the national touring company of a Broadway show, we opened in Chicago, and after a month's run, we traveled by train with trunk loads of costumes and a railcar of sets and scenery to San Francisco for the next months' run. Opening night, I learned the hard way that each stage can have small inconsistencies in how the set realigns with a particular proscenium. While executing a cartwheel, which I had done for several months on other stages and in dance studios, I attempted, in midair, to avoid hitting the set and threw my back out as I landed. This also illustrates that injuries often occur when trying to avoid them. Don't put your hands down to break your fall. That's a likely way to break your wrist.

Crawling off the stage was painful but not out of character for the jester part I was playing. But the injury would take several months of PT to recover from, so the tears I shed were partly over my expectation that I would be fired from my job. I wasn't.

The dance captain and the director came up with a generous and blessed solution, which they got the whole company to participate in. I was given more lines of dialogue and traded my more physically challenging dance parts for less athletic dance roles, while other cast members covered for me on the parts I couldn't do. Talk about having the support of your community! It was an example of what the theatre arts do for those who participate in them as performers. The generosity and joy of working together to create something bigger than oneself, something that cannot happen alone.

A half a century later, on one unseasonably warm spring morning, as I traveled across the studio dance floor in a sideward motion, instead of sliding smoothly, my feet began sticking to the floor and I couldn't get them under me soon enough to avoid a crash landing directly on my left shoulder onto the wooden floor. The sound and sensation left little doubt that something had broken. Though I hated to delay the class, I refused to allow anyone to move me until the emergency personnel came with the stretcher.

At the hospital, the doctor confirmed, "You broke your shoulder in two places, but you didn't misalign it. So don't pull it out and you won't need surgery." In an office consultation a few days later, I carefully worded my question. "What am I *risking* by using the plane ticket I have already purchased to fly to Nebraska to attend my granddaughter's high school graduation at the end of this week?" He helped my husband and me strategize how to maneuver me in a wheelchair through airports and airplane aisles so my shoulder didn't get bumped.

I didn't have to tell him that my determination to attend Tori's graduation sprang from the fact that Tori's mother endured painful treatments for breast cancer from the time Tori was four years old until she was seven. While the cancer threatened her life, she kept the goal of living long enough to be present at Tori's high school graduation. She died five days after Tori's seventh birthday. There was no way I was going to miss this graduation.

Though this incident happened over ten years ago, it continues to teach me something that we can experience when we have a loss or a dramatic injury. Perhaps we could call it a "what if" moment. In the early weeks or months after the injury, my mind would spontaneously take me back to the few minutes when I was enroute to the dance studio that fateful morning.

Just after I turned off my street, I saw that I would need to take a different route to the studio because the street I would normally take had been blocked to accommodate a marathon community run. I attempted to follow the signs, but I was annoyed. It was a Sunday and I thought, "Maybe I don't have to go to class today. I go several times a week. I'm likely to be late anyway." But being the determined, disciplined person that I am, I overrode that thought, overcame the difficulties presented, and went to the class.

It took me probably close to a year of hard work and physical therapy exercises to be able to raise my left arm as high as my right. During that time, especially when I was tired or discouraged, this memory of that choice point would come to me.

If only I had listened to that voice none of this would have been necessary. I think of these "what if" moments as instances of our brains spiraling back to the point where a different action on our part would have insured a more desirable outcome. For example, if we had not driven to the grocery store that evening, we wouldn't have had that car accident. As we grieve amidst this reality we do not prefer, we must let go, again and again, of that road we didn't travel and deal with the one we are on.

Aging

The nuns refer to their experiences of aging as "diminishments." In InterPlay, we remind one another to go the speed of our bodies. Not the body we had yesterday or the one we are hoping to have tomorrow, but the one we have today, whatever condition it may be in. There can be perceptible physical losses as we age. I saw more walkers and wheelchairs in the convent dining room than we ever saw when these sisters were teaching in our schools. Instead of running or hurrying about, elders walk more slowly, more deliberately. I've given up running up and down the stairs, and my husband and I have promised one another that we will hold onto the stair railings as we transport items up and down in our house. Falls are more likely now and their effect more costly. The one that doesn't fall has to be the caregiver of the other.

To open a jar, we have a tool in a kitchen drawer that helps get a better grip on its lid. Friends limit their driving to daylight hours, or prefer side streets to faster, more crowded freeways. And of course, if eyesight falters, or reaction time slows, or anxiety heightens, it may be time to surrender the car keys. Big city folks with reliable public transportation sometimes never learned to drive. And young people now prefer Uber, Lyft, or renting a bicycle to get around.

But it's the mental losses we fear the most, along with the self-identity that we are used to being seen as capable and skilled. Names are hard to recall, even the names of people we know well. Among my friends, we tease that it takes three people to finish a sentence, excluding the pause to Google a name or date or fact check someone else's pronouncements. But there's an Italian saying, "At the table, one does not age." When people slow down, put their screens away, relax, go the speed of their bodies, and enjoy a meal with friends and family, the dial on the stress clock stops.

You might not come to this conclusion automatically in our youth-obsessed culture, but a long life is a blessing. If a person is aging well, they have probably stopped sweating the small stuff. They've stopped taking life for granted and learned to appreciate the time left. As a person's future shortens, whether due to age or illness, the present moment becomes more important as that's the place where joy, beauty, and love reside. As the priest and author, Richard Rohr suggests, "There is suffering and loss in the second half of life—in fact, maybe even more. But there is now a changed capacity to hold it creatively with less anxiety."

I was looking at a photograph on my dresser and realized that of the eight women and girls sitting on the front stoop of the house I grew up in, I am the only one left on this earth. Longer life often involves being the one left behind. I thought of our Aunt Dote, who was the last one standing in the family in her generation, which surprised her greatly given all the diseases she suffered from. "I'm gonna stop going to the doctors," she said at one time in her mid-eighties. "Every time I go, they give me a new disease." As she approached ninety, she would say, "Why am I still here? Why am I still here?" She seemed a very young child asking me why the sky is blue or why are raindrops wet. I never could come up with a good answer. Rohr compared an authentic life to what "Eastern Orthodoxy believed about authentic religious art. It would always have a bright sadness to it."

In 1957, the year I graduated high school, the cartoonist Jules Feiffer created a skinny, pony-tailed, barefooted modern dancer as a lead character for his cartoon strip. For the next forty years, the dancer's ebullient, dramatic gyrations expressed the highs and lows of the political and social issues of the time until Feiffer retired her, and himself, in 2000. My favorite strip of the dancer was one that summarized all the others, and that I believe expresses, in a nutshell, the ubiquitous challenge of physical and emotional illness, injuries, disabilities, and diminishments. Come with me as I dance the strip's separate squares.

99

First frame: *Life is Worth Living!!!*

I flail my arms over my head in all directions in total abandonment, lift one foot at a time, jump into the air, an ecstatic smile on my face, alternating with stomping movements into the earth, like a tap dancer or a flamenco performer with arms overhead playing castanets.

Second Frame: *Life is NOT worth living!!!*

I clutch my chest, my upper body bends forward, causing my arms to hang listlessly towards the ground. I begin to allow my head to roll to the side and backwards, initiating a spiral path. Eyes closed, my head rolls back, and as it completes the circular spiral, it slumps forward towards the ground. I grasp the sides of my head with the palms of my hands and breathe a deep sign of dejection.

Third Frame: *I dance to perfect both answers!!!*

I raise both arms in a balletic circle over my head and joining the thumb and middle finger on each hand, open the circle to reach my arms out to the side, assuming a centered yogic pose. As I cross one foot in front of the other, I drop my arms and cross them in front of my body while continuing to hold my fingers in the mudra. As the final caption is said or read, I open my palms upward.

Artist Resource

The Isolation Journals, born of the pandemic and the health challenges of its founder, writer Suleika Jaquad—who has undergone two bone marrow transplants—is an online community that encourages the practice of journaling for its paid and free subscribers. The site includes a newsletter for people seeking to transform life's interruptions into creative grist. It's a great place to receive support and inspiration when you are dealing with the life interruptions that illness and its treatments create.

Reflection/Action

1. Remember an experience of an illness or injury that you've had in your life, or an experience of companioning a loved one through an illness or injury. What lessons did these experiences teach you? Were their gifts at the episode's end, or later in reflecting on them?

2. What music did you play during that time of your health challenge or that of your loved ones' challenge? My son Ken's favorite was Seasons of Love from the musical Rent. It asks the question: how do you measure a year in a life? My daughter Corinne's favorite song was For Good from the musical Wicked. It suggests that people (and experiences) bring into our lives something we must learn and concludes that "I'm who I am today because I knew you, and I'm changed for good." See if you can identify a song or a poem that might provide inspiration or encouragement for you or a loved one when going through an episode of illness, injury, treatment, and recovery.

Chapter Seven

Estrangement: Broken Hearts, Families, and Careers

When my family puts together a memorial, photography is one of the arts we rely on. In the old days, family members brought their favorite snapshots to the gathering, and whomever was hosting secured large sheets of posterboard and glue sticks to fasten the photos onto it. "Be sure and mark the back with your name so you can get your photos back when we take the display down," someone would suggest.

By the time I was preparing for my sister Pat's memorial in the spring of 2021, I had recent photos on my phone. But to find the developed snapshots from our childhood, I would have to go through a trunk in our storage container, which I was dreading. Fortunately, Pat's son Adam sent me a digital file that he had made of all the photos he found among his mother's belongings. There were images I had never seen, especially one of a person I knew about but had never met.

The photo was from the mid-sixties and was of Pat's first love—a handsome, dark-skinned man whom she met when they were both students at a college in Kalamazoo, Michigan. This man and his relationship with Pat was how my siblings and I found out about our usually logical, fair-minded father's racism. We looked at one another aghast when our dad exhibited a totally unanticipated dramatic outburst upon learning that his daughter had a relationship with a Black man. Later, we asked one another how we did not know this—all his comments on daily news stories in his precious newspaper, all that talking back to the television set. Did he know that's how *he* felt?

Dad's attitude was non-negotiable and meant that Pat was never able to bring this man into our home. I'm sure my sister treasured the images Adam found of him and their beautiful daughter, given up for adoption at birth, partly to spare all of them the pain of family engagements and estrangements.

Estrangement involves treating someone as an unwelcome stranger, often in a relationship where former closeness and affection existed. Adult children risk estrangement from a parent if they choose a relationship, like my sister did, with someone deemed unacceptable, from the "wrong" religion, racial, or ethnic group. Our own parents' family members were unwelcoming to their Catholic-Protestant "mixed marriage." Their weddings could not take place in a church but in the priest's rectory.

Parents may become estranged from their children over issues leftover from the parents' divorce, such as when children are made to feel the need to sides with one parent or the other, or if grown children have memories of child abuse or resentments stemming from what they now see as neglect. Sometimes, parents fail to let go of the control over their offspring they once had when their children were young. The grief that accompanies such circumstances springs from the human need to belong, to be loved and accepted, despite our failings and our differences.

When I was in early bereavement after the death of each of my adult children, I reminded myself of what I knew as a social worker: that losing a loved one to death is not the worst or most difficult way to lose a loved one. I've known clients whose children were in prison after years of disengagement from the family, or years of bad behavior that caused family members to disengage from them. Adult children can be lost to their family members through drug addiction or untreated mental illness, as can a family elder.

I know people whose adult children no longer speak to them or allow them to see their grandchildren. Other clients have had parents who "disowned" them because of who they married, who they love, how they worship, or vote. And then there are the familiar dramatic lines of being disowned, "I no longer have a son!" Or "You are dead to me!" These lines work best on stage and television dramas if the actor also states their intention to disinherit the relative.

Estrangement from a family member is one of the most painful life experiences according to Karl Pellemer, author of the book *Fault Lines: Fractured Families and How to Mend Them*, yet this type of loss has not been on most people's radar until relatively recently. From his ten-year research on the issue in his Cornell Reconciliation Project, Pellemer estimates that more than sixty-five million people suffer from such riffs. Another author, Kylie Agllias, in her book *Family Estrangement: A Matter of Perspective*, looks at these losses that **feel like a death** through the lens of Attachment Theory, Bowen Family Systems Theory, and theories of grief and loss. "Whilst data suggests that around 1 in 12 people are estranged from at least one family member, this topic is rarely discussed or researched."

I was attending seminars in my field as a family therapist during a time when I was going through marital difficulties in my first marriage. One of my teachers, whose name I've forgotten, said something that I've never forgotten: "You will never be rid of someone you have ever loved." I found this wisdom both depressing and hopeful at the same time.

This is telling us that emotional cut-offs don't work. The disowning—"I have no son!"—is a lie, and likely an expression of the speaker's anger and disappointment at their son. He is not dead, though perhaps does not now resemble the person that his parents raised. There is a need to grieve what they had hoped for in their son, and for the kind of relationship they had imagined they would be able to have with him.

Take the situation where it seems love itself has died. Let's just call it the "Big D." Since fifty percent of marital relationships fail, we don't want to say it out loud, lest it come true. Maybe you're a child being kept awake by the angry voices of your parents fighting late into the night, or a depressed husband who doesn't want to talk about how he feels because he would have to admit he just doesn't want to be married anymore, or a young wife, like I was, who would have done anything to not have to raise three young children as a single mom. The grief literature tells us love never dies, but in long-term committed relationships, it's sometimes hard to find evidence that love is still there.

In the film, *Love Story*, the oft-quoted line, "Love means never having to say you're sorry," is not true, but the person most responsible for your sorrow may no longer be willing to hear you express it. Sometimes, loving someone can mean you have to say goodbye, or loosen the bonds of connection and have less contact, especially if you hope to be able to continue loving and taking care of yourself.

Popular Songs Grieve the Loss of Love

Partnerships, friendships, particularly romantic relationships, and marriages sometimes need to end or be reconfigured. Mutually coming to that determination is rare, but through the years, pop and country songs have provided some wisdom for our grieving. In 1960, Neil Sedaka made it clear that "breaking up is hard to do." Neil sings the part of the one who isn't ready: "Don't take your love away from me/ don't say this is the end/ wish we were making up/ starting anew," all followed by a catchy "du be do be do."

Sometimes what we want is not to end a relationship but to change it. Fifty-one million people have viewed Taylor Swift's video *You Belong With Me*, about a relationship moving from friends to lovers, "Dreaming about the day when you wake up and find/ that what you're looking for has been here the whole time." But what about a change in the opposite direction? I'm sure you're familiar with that dreaded phrase men and boys hate, that a woman or girl might say when she breaks up with him: "I just want us to be friends." Rather than a put down, if she really means it, a friendship that lasts can be one of the most important relationships throughout a person's lifetime — part of what we sometimes refer to as "our family of choice." I couldn't find songs about a relationship trying to change in that direction — from lovers to friends, from relatives to friends, despite this being a much-needed transition for divorcing couples attempting to co-parent their children.

In her 1984 hit song *What's Love Got to Do With it?* Tina Turner highlighted a notion that was just emerging in our culture as a serious problem at that time. Domestic violence. Four years after she extricated herself from a twenty-three-year relationship with her mentor and husband Ike Turner, a relationship that began when she was sixteen years old, she sang, "Who needs a heart when a heart can be broken/ I've been taking a new direction/ thinking about my own protection."

Then, of course, there are plenty of they-done-me wrong songs. "Cry me a river/ I've cried a river over you." And many hang-in-there-no-matter-what songs, like *Stand by Your Man*, which I always found particularly annoying. But playing the role of either victim, persecutor, or rescuer is not advised lest we set ourselves up to replay, in the new relationship, the dynamics of the one just ending.

When songwriter Miley Cyrus and Australian actor Liam Harmsworth's five-year relationship ended, the song she wrote about it, *Flowers*, broke all records as number one on the three different Billboard charts. Three years after their divorce, the song ignited a social media storm as fans questioned its true meaning and decided that Miley must be seeking revenge given the fact that she released *Flowers* on Liam's birthday.

I can't speak to Miley's motives, but I see evidence of wisdom not manifest in earlier break up songs. Cyrus begins with "We were good, we were gold/ kinda dream that can't be sold/ we were right till we weren't/ built a home and watched it burn." Fans know that building a home and watching it burn did actually happen shortly before their breakup, and I'm aware that a loss of such magnitude changes people and the relationships they are in. Miley sings of her reaction, "Didn't want to leave, didn't want to fight, started to cry, but then..." she reminds herself, "I can buy myself flowers/ talk to myself for hours/say things you don't understand/take myself dancing/hold my own hand." And the line of wisdom I greatly appreciate and have never heard in any song, "I can **love me** better than you can." I appreciate Miley teaching all her fans the truth that our first obligation is to ourselves and that we can only love someone else and accept love from them to the extent that we love ourselves. Perhaps we need more songs with repetition and rhythm that can help us get this truth into our bones.

A Divorce Ritual

Divorce is one of the most challenging of life's transitions, unlike a death, where there are rituals and community practices that support the person's moving through it, no such cultural rituals exist when relationships end or transform. I found when leading a women's movement therapy group that people can construct their own rituals. One of our members, call her Susan, was getting her second divorce, and when I asked her if she wanted to create a divorce ritual like the ones we'd done for other group members, she surprised me by saying, "Oh, no. I've got this divorcing thing down. It's the marrying thing. I have pledged my love and devotion to two men, and neither situation worked out well for me. I need to marry myself!"

Though I'd never heard of it, I took her up on her idea. I gave her a worksheet on which to plan out some elements to include in her ritual and she came back the next week and directed us in how to help her enact a ritual to marry herself. Susan borrowed items from the children's play therapy room, finger puppets and small toys to create a bouquet to carry, and a crown and a red cape to wear. Each woman selected a colorful scarf to drape over themselves and dance with as they accompanied Susan in a procession to the altar where she insisted on walking backwards. Guided by the group's directions, she was able to stay mindful of the path she had taken to get there. All those pledges she made to those men, "to have and to hold, to love and cherish, in wealth and in poverty, in sickness and health," she made to herself, "till death ends my life." And like what often happens at the end of wedding ceremonies, the group members danced wildly into the night.

This movement and theatrical enactment is an example of how the arts can help us process loss and challenging life experiences. We were fortunate to have a children's play therapy room nearby to borrow objects and costumes from and to have adult women willing to use their playful imaginations as children so often naturally do. When seeking behavioral changes, behaving or actually doing something registers differently in the brain than just talking about it or imagining it.

Avoiding War

It's a type of war that creates many family estrangements, where beloved ones become "the enemy." Such hostilities are frequently created when people use the courts to settle disputes or realign their relationships. While I was a professor of social work at the university, I collaborated on a journal article with a family lawyer on what women going through a divorce need to know. Rather than the adversarial tools of *my lawyer can beat up your lawyer*, we maintained that what is needed is a way to craft a win-win solution. In intimate relationships, a win-lose is a lose-lose for the relationship and all parties.

I knew this well, having worked with many women going through divorce. As soon as lawyers got involved, the women were totally blindsided when their once gentle, loving partner began behaving as a *go-for-the-jugular* opponent. Stunned by this personality change, the women would go from shock to despair, often questioning themselves and their choice of getting connected to this horrid person in the first place.

After fourteen years of marriage, I had to admit with great sorrow that though I had helped many client couples repair their relationships, I could not do the same for my own. Going through a divorce in Nebraska in 1975 while being a family therapist, I couldn't do what I knew was best and involve a counselor as a mediator to help us resolve our differences. "That's not *my* thing, that's *your* thing," my husband said. I knew I couldn't play all the roles necessary in the mediation process—the objective third party, the wife, and the mother—at the same time, so all I could do was convince my husband that we use a single lawyer. Legally, a lawyer cannot represent both parties, so we worked out the details and then my lawyer drew them up and filed them.

My work with families had shown me the risk to our three children and ourselves if we pursued an adversarial process through the courts. The children had already endured our nearly two-year separation during which they moved between two homes. They had shown strong signs of their own grief. When I finally told thirteen-year-old Corinne our decision to divorce, she said quietly, with a sigh, "I've cried a thousand tears already." Eleven-year-old Kevin put on a tough front, telling me his plan, which was to get his own apartment as soon as possible. The one he chose was conveniently located in the new building of small apartments being built next door to my house. And nine-year-old Kenny teared up often at our family meetings, crying on behalf of *all* of us it seemed to me.

I was able to convince my husband that, for the sake of our children, even though we couldn't make a good marriage, we could dedicate ourselves to making a good divorce. We appeared in court, only to be sent away. "I am not convinced that everything has been done to save this marriage," the judge said. "This couple have three children and are asking for joint custody. They are represented by one lawyer and are planning to hold property in common. I am sending them to court-ordered family mediation," he said as he tapped his gavel on the podium.

We finally got to where I wanted to be, but it was too late. The divorce was finally granted when the counseling session turned up what are called "irreconcilable differences." When the counselor asked me what I would gain by getting a divorce, I said something like, "I enjoyed being married, and someday, if I get a divorce, I'd be able to marry again." George said, "Oh, that's the last thing I would want."

Hopefully, there are more processes in place now to support people as they transform their family structures into a now common two household arrangement. Our good divorce worked out well, especially for our children, as we were able to remain friendly partners while parenting. Once our children became parents themselves, they often mentioned their gratitude for the efforts we, and their stepdad Rich, made to create and maintain a blended family where we all felt we belonged.

Work Estrangements

Forty percent of people will lose a job at least once in their lifetime and twenty-three percent of people will lose a job three or more times, according to data from Intoo and the Harris Poll. In being fired, laid off, or furloughed, seventy-three percent of people will experience anxiety. This easily understandable anxiety may be increased or decreased in intensity depending on how much money you have in savings, whether this loss also means the loss of your health insurance or a need to relocate to a place with more opportunities, and what kind of connections and skills you have to secure another position. It also matters if the industry you are in or the national or global economy is expanding or contracting, or if the cost of living is rising. But let's shine a light on something mostly overlooked regarding career downturns and job losses: estrangement.

Freud called love and work, "cornerstones of our humanness." Many people spend at least as much of their awake time at work as they do outside of it. Social relationship networks form around work assignments, identities are forged and reinforced around job titles and acquired skills. So, to no longer be on friendly terms, to be escorted out of the building by a security officer, to have lost closeness and affection and the support of co-workers, perhaps respect from members of your profession, is to be suffering the grief of estrangement. As with every type of loss, to grieve it, it's important to be able to name it.

The year was 1997. Our youngest son Kenneth had died in June on the summer solstice, and the sale of our family business was finalized in mid-July of that same year. As we were signing the papers (which also corresponded with my birthday), the owner/manager of the company who purchased us, who happened to be a social worker, said, "So much grief, Sheila. Seems like a lot, all at the same time." It was a lot.

I felt like I was sleepwalking in a cloud of overwhelm. So much of what I had put my energy into—the clinic that had been the fulfillment of my career dream after having to let go of university teaching—had become a nightmare to operate under the changes in the payment structures of the healthcare industry. We had to let go of our independence and become part of a larger organization to survive. The fact that there were no women in leadership roles in the purchasing organization did not feel hopeful for my career. With all this coming so soon after my son's death, it seemed I was having to say goodbye to much of what had given my life meaning, much of what I had loved.

It is customary for the leadership of a company to stay on for several years after being acquired, which we did, but since the company had little idea of what my role had been in making the business something they wanted to purchase, they didn't ask for my counsel, and I focused on my provider role of seeing patients. After eighteen months, the company owner took me to lunch and asked if we would like to buy the clinic back. My husband stayed on in his management role, but we respectfully declined. Soon after, I resigned to become a caregiver to my daughter Corinne as she underwent a bone marrow transplant.

When Work and Family Connections Combine

Now that we appreciate that estrangements can happen in families and in work settings, I'd like to offer my husband Rich's family as an example of what can happen when the family connections also involve the family business, particularly when people turn to the courts.

Rich had always known that his father, Jack, who was the youngest member of a "his, hers, and ours" family structure, carried much sorrow and unhappiness over the fact that many of his close relatives refused any communication with him after both of his parents died. The estrangement lasted through the second half of Jack's life, keeping his children from knowing many of their relatives or having any clear idea of what caused this family rift in the first place.

After Rich's mother died, I was given the job of cleaning out her closet as we prepared to put her condo on the market. In its dark recesses, behind the shoes and the less frequently worn hanging formal clothes, I found a dusty two-hundred-page blue booklet. It was a transcript of a legal case tried before the New York State Supreme Court in the early fifties. Family members and their heirs challenged the will of Jack's mother, which dictated how funds from the family business were to be distributed.

Long before the court case, Jack left the family business over conflicts with his older brothers and their image of "real" work. They didn't think his focus on researching, writing, and securing government contracts for the family's wholesale paint business should exempt him from helping them load and unload fifty-gallon paint cans every day. This conflict with his brothers caused Jack, in his early forties, to take a financial payout that he was entitled to at that time and invested it in a retail paint store. He and his wife ran the store while he studied for his new career as a stockbroker. All of Jack's brothers died in their fifties, and by the time of the lawsuit, it was their wives and descendants who were involved, along with two of Jack's sisters.

Richard and his two brothers had been told that there was a court battle around the time Rich was born and that its outcome had changed the laws of the state of New York regarding inheritance. Here were the details in this booklet in the back of the dark closet; details of the long-kept family secret—who said what in response to what questions under oath. There were thirteen attorneys listed on the cover of the transcript, which supported what Rich and his brothers had been told: that most all the money went to the lawyers and people outside the family when the matter was finally settled. Reading this document, it was easy to understand why family relationships did not survive the damage those hostile proceedings caused. It also helped to explain why Jack and his wife had so much trouble accepting the children I brought into the family. Unresolved grief does not always end in the generation it is created.

To Whom Do We Belong?

One way to characterize these estrangements and losses, whether they involve loved ones or beloved work and careers, is the loss of a sense of belonging. According to one of my teachers and mentors, Cynthia Winton-Henry, these "patterns of sorrow can create despair. To whom do I belong and who belongs to me begins and ends with a soul connection. This connection is inseparable from the infinite ground-sky of the Ultimate Source, God, Love, whatever you call it."

Sometimes we call it "being a part of something larger than ourselves," and like grieving many kinds of loss, being able to set aside our shame and speak of what has happened allows us to support one another and compare notes on ways to heal. An art-based structure can help us share the stories in a ritual container that removes the stigma and honors the losses and the pain we have endured while also providing a way to process it.

The simple ritual structure involves collecting our stories around a theme, in this case, *To Whom Do We Belong and Who Belongs to Us?* The question is stated and followed by a story. The question is repeated, and another story is offered. This can be a solo process done by oneself in writing or a group process with different people taking turns telling their own individual stories on the theme as they address the question. This is the format that follows in this art-based example.

To Whom Do We Belong and Who Belongs to Us?

Family therapists often say that "families are only as sick as their secrets," and a death can sometimes reveal what some of these secrets have been. In the Irish culture of my mother's ancestors, when a person is near death and family members gather to connect and console one another, this time is described as the "thin time"—the time when the veil between the worlds is lifted, and important truths and long kept secrets are often revealed.

As my son Kenneth lay in a hospital bed in our living room, now transformed into the dying room, relatives gather on the sun porch. I overhear their discussion of my younger brother, Kenneth, whom I named my son after. They speak of his disappearance, and the recovery of his body by hunters nearly two years later. Eavesdropping from the other room, I learn details and facts I'd never heard anyone speak of— facts my mother had gone to her grave not knowing. There are taboos against talking about such matters, like the fact that the bullet hole in the back of his head confirmed that he had been murdered. My brother-in-law, in his visit to the area (which I knew nothing about), talked with several people who knew what had transpired. "We thought they were just gonna teach him a lesson, rough him up a bit," a local fella told him. The coroner's report did discern that the gun had been fired at close range, indicating for certain his death had been an execution. What kind of misunderstanding? What kind of offense could lead to this? And how could our peace-loving brother, a conscientious objector who did alternative service during the Vietnam War come to such an end? And how could our Irish-Catholic mother ever reconcile this with her understanding of how God works? The truth is, she never did.

To Whom Do We Belong and Who Belongs to Us?

One of the happiest days in my sister Pat's life was when her daughter Lynn, at the age of thirty, found her. My sister called me and was breathless trying to contain her excitement, "The most wonderful thing has happened!" I remember thinking, *she's met a new guy? She's won the lottery? She wouldn't get this excited over a guy or money,* but when she told me about Lynn finding her–I wasn't surprised that they talked for eight hours non-stop on the phone to "meet one another and catch up."

After that call, many members of Pat's family got to meet Lynn, and through our discussions, we seemed to help Lynn accept some of the things about herself that were different from her adoptive family. "Seems I'm always late, and all the members of my family are very prompt." We admitted, "Except for Dad, most of us have trouble getting anywhere on time." It had taken Lynn a long time to finish college and she seemed encouraged by the fact that her mother and her first cousin on our side of the family each took ten years to complete their degrees.

We got to meet her parents, who were gracious and welcoming, her mother accompanying her to Dad's funeral. I had hoped that Lynn would consider herself a member of our family, but after a year or so, she stopped responding to our invitations and letters. I had the sense that her curiosity about who and where she came from was satisfied by meeting her birth mother and some of the family, but going forward she did not want to belong to us or have us belong to her.

Pat had a much more spacious acceptance of that decision than I did. I do still hope that she came to understand that given the racist attitudes of the U.S. culture at the time, not to mention those of members of our own family, it was her mother's deep love for her that caused her to surrender any claim on Lynn as soon as she found a family who could give her what Pat could not—an accepting, loving family and community. Sometimes loving someone means we must let them go.

To Whom Do We Belong and Who Belongs to Us?

National efforts to raise awareness of spousal, domestic, and dating violence began in 1987, though my awareness of this issue began in the early eighties. A woman professor, a mentor of mine, and a person I very much admired told me of her volunteer work on the board of one of the first women's shelters in the country. When I asked this brilliant, articulate woman how she got involved, she told me that she had been an abused wife. This blew my mind. She did not fit my image of a person who might be involved in such a situation.

Hopefully, in the nearly forty years since congress passed Public Law 101-112, officially designating October as National Domestic Violence Awareness Month, we have become more aware and more understanding of what domestic violence is, who can be its victims, how pervasive it is in our culture, how it involves and affects workplaces, and, especially, ways to address it. But through the years, one of the most difficult issues to understand is expressed in this question: *why doesn't she just leave?* The issues are complex. As I've looked more closely at family estrangements of all types, I believe that looking at partner violence through the lens of grief provides some answers—answers that apply to other situations of family estrangement as well.

People in close relationships often reveal themselves to one another, and see one another, at their best and at their worst. Sometimes, these aspects are not well integrated with one another, so it seems like the person is two people. One day, the person you met and fell in love with, or the person you raised, or knew in a positive way for years begins treating you as an enemy and the source of all their unhappiness. Later, perhaps they apologize or, even if they don't, they seem to regret their behavior and begin treating you in a more positive way. Now it seems the person you love has returned and you reinvest in the relationship. And then, the cycle begins all over again.

Some of us, myself included, have a hard time giving up on those we love or on the relationship we had with them in the past. We hang in there way longer than what others would see as making good sense. We stay in jobs longer than we should for our own good. We give people more chances to change, or to keep their promises.

I was separated for several years before finally taking the steps to divorce, hoping beyond hope that I wouldn't have to divorce. If the person dies, we are forced to separate. As my student Marti, a young widow, told me when I told her I envied her, "It is easier in some ways when the person dies. I have the positive memories of my husband and our relationship, and I don't have to be concerned about running into him at the grocery store with his new wife."

The Way Forward

It's said that grief is love with nowhere to go. When the object of love is no longer available to receive love, or it is unsafe for the griever's wellbeing to get close enough to offer it, with the support of compassionate friends and family members the griever must turn love toward themselves. Now, they are the one most in need of love.

When the loved one has turned away, exhibiting indifference which is what Holocaust survivor and Nobel Laureat Elie Wiesel sees as the opposite of love, or when a person must limit contact or closeness for their own sake, then self-love and acceptance of love from others form the necessary healing potion. Like grieving many other kinds of loss, removing the stigma is necessary to support one another and compare notes on ways to heal the devastation of intimate loss. The process is to forgive ourselves for whatever part we played in the estrangement, whether in family or work settings. We may have done everything right and still none of it worked. Then be open to the support of a loving community, as we would receive if our loved one had died. Next, to reconfigure a new life without the person or the type of relationship we formerly had. And through all this, to use the arts to help us hold onto the hope that whatever happens in the future, the memories of what began in love still belong to us.

Artist Resource

The theme of when something you love ends—that time to let go of a relationship, a job, a dream, a life—is ubiquitous in popular songs of many eras. Watch the story song by Billie Eilish performed by The Bengsons, a married couple themselves, titled *When the Party's Over*. Notice it's not just about the words or the tune.

121

Reflection/Action

1. Describe a person you once loved who, though still living, is no longer in your life. What did your relationship with that person teach you? What was your gift to them?

2. Try the ritual storytelling framework of stating the question *to whom do I belong and who belongs to me?* followed by a snippet of a story of your own experience. Repeat several times, and then read out loud what you have created.

Chapter Eight

Death: Celebrating Life and Love to the End

The short story writer and playwright William Soroyan died of cancer in a veteran's hospital at the age of seventy-two. His 1981 obituary in *The Washington Post* contained a quote from an interview he gave the *Associated Press* shortly after the onset of his final illness. "Everybody has got to die, but I have always believed an exception would be made in my case. Now what?"

In another example of wit and gallows humor, poet and theater critic Dorothy Parker left an interesting suggestion for her tombstone, "Wherever she went, including here, it was against her better judgment."

Most of us, if we're honest with ourselves, can identify with the attitude behind Saroyan's and Parker's self-deprecating comments. Despite early advice from such masters as Socrates that we "practice dying," most of us in Western culture distract ourselves, through way-too-busy lives, from the fact of our own inevitable demise. Another writer, Ernest Hemingway, reminds us of something that is important to remember: "All stories, if continued far enough, end in death and he is no true storyteller who would keep that from you."

As I've gotten older, the reality of my own death comes into my awareness more frequently, often through mundane activities, like my recent attempts to tidy my home. Friends told me of a practice from Sweden called "Death Cleaning," which got me started. Author Margareta Magussen, who coined the term, suggests that "getting rid of items can serve as a reminder that things don't last forever, including us." Downsizing seems a kind of rightsizing to me now as I sell one home and declutter another, letting go of too much abundance, finding people who could use whatever I no longer need, and figuring out a proper place for items I am keeping. In this process, I feel lighter with less, and with knowing that when I leave, loved ones will have less mess to contend with.

I got this connection between decluttering and death when I became a student of Melody LeBaron. A person who pays a great deal of attention to the spaces where we live and work, she was offering an online class to help people declutter their homes and workspaces. Most people in the class were, like me, having trouble letting go of our "treasures," yet we often live with people that have little regard for objects, either letting them pile up and not noticing the piles, or tossing them out without a thought. Seinfeld has a great comedy routine where he tells us what side of that dichotomy he's on: "The wedding album? I thought you were through with that."

When I learned that Melody was a death doula, accompanying people as they let go of this life, I began to look at this dance of how we treat our living spaces and the objects in them from a larger perspective. Her book, *Transforming Death: Creating Sacred Space for the Dying*, suggests a reframing and renaming of death and offers guidance on creating sacred space for the dying and its gifts to the living.

A diagnosis or a health challenge often brings our mortality to mind, like it did when my phone rang recently.

124

My eighty-one-year-old brother Miles was on the line from New Mexico. He called from the intensive care room where he was being treated after a medical incident involving his heart. He had been ready to go home, but now he says he must stay under observation as he tries out a medicine the doctors think he needs.

Our conversation gave both of us confirmation that all we really have is the present moment. We talk about not wanting another family funeral so soon after our sister's last month. This leads us to a strong desire to call on help from other realms. In our family, that means calling kid sister Maureen, the best pray-er in our bunch. I called Maureen to let her know the situation, and while I'm on the phone with her, she begins talking directly to God. "Dear God, here we are, two or more gathered in your name. We know you will hear our prayer. We call to your attention our brother Miles. Even though Miles can be extremely aggravating and annoying, we'd like to have him stay around a while longer, if it be your will." It seems it was God's will because Miles is still with us.

Buddhists see staying aware of our impermanence as a way to appreciate life more fully. We might not spend so much time on things that don't matter and have more gratitude for what does come our way. I remember reading somewhere that the Dalai Lama sets an alarm (might be once an hour) to remind him to stop and contemplate his own death. To my Western mind, this seemed a rather morbid practice until I learned of a Bhutanese folk saying: "In order to be a happy person, one must contemplate death five times a day."

Following through on this concept, I learned that Bhutan has become well known worldwide for their measurement of what they call their Gross National Happiness (GNH). Proposed at the United Nations in 1998 as an alternative way to measure development rather than the Gross National Product (GNP), this country randomly selects and interviews a sample of their 800,000-person population. Eventually, they began measuring more than just whether people meditate on death and they've spawned a global industry on measuring happiness.

Following breadcrumbs like these on Google, I learned of an easy way to try out regularly meditating on death. Turns out, there's an app for that. Buddhist marketing expert, Hansa Bergwall, created the *WeCroak* smartphone app, which sends recipients five quotes of encouragement throughout the day to live more mindfully, inviting them to stop and think about death. Bergwall sees "death contemplation" as the next step in practicing mindfulness, and thousands of subscribers like me are giving it a try. Find happiness by contemplating your mortality at wecroak.com.

Is Dying an Art We Can Get Good At?

Before his execution by the state, Socrates gave his students a piece of advice. "Practice dying," he told them as he was facing his own death. He didn't say, "Don't forget you are going to die." He said "practice" the process. He believed that through the process of dying a person would most likely obtain the wisdom that they had been seeking all their lives and that the philosopher's soul is purified, resulting in a moral maturity. This reminds me of an expression that I believe, better than anything else, defines a person as a grown up: "What I want changes when I see what the situation requires."

What does the process of dying require? Let's turn to a masterful poet to help us answer that question.

A Poet's Wisdom

To live in this world
You must be able
to do three things:
to love what is mortal,
        to hold it

against your bones knowing
your own life depends on it;
and, when the time comes to let it
go,
        to let it go.

-Mary Oliver, *In Blackwater Woods*

As I was leaving to accompany my friend Rose as she was dying, another friend, Jyoti, shared with me wisdom from her experiences as a midwife, accompanying women as they give birth. "When life is coming in and when life is going out, those are the times of the greatest light." These times are referred to by the ancients as the "time between the worlds," or what the Irish call the "thin time," when the veil between the worlds is lifted. Elements of the mystery may emerge, issues may be resolved, and truths clarified.

When the pain that often accompanies these processes can be managed properly, we are given the opportunity to experience these transition times as we are accompanying a loved one or are being accompanied ourselves. I often hear people say, "I'm not afraid of death, but dying really scares me." Following that comment, they usually say something that amounts to, "I can't handle pain," or "I don't want to suffer."

If we stay with this connection between the coming in and the going out of life, some wisdom emerges. In both instances, the technologies of modern medicine carry the potential for facilitating or for overwhelming these natural processes. What were once home and family-centered life events became, in the first half of the twentieth century, managed and determined by medical experts. While offering relief from pain, medical interventions often prolonged the processes or, in making the person unconscious, robbed them of the experience.

As for the birthing process, when my father, who was born in 1912, was growing up on an Illinois farm, no one said the taboo word "pregnant." Preparations and birth announcements amounted to his oldest sister saying to the youngest one, "Mary's gonna need you next week, Bertha," followed by, "Pass the potatoes," at the dinner table.

When pregnant with me, my nurse-mother enlisted all the latest medical advances of the late thirties and did not wake up for several days after she birthed me. There was no pain, but no experience of birthing a child either. When I became pregnant in the second half of the twentieth century, I chose to become part of a worldwide movement of "natural" or "prepared" childbirth, where women and their partners learned about the process of childbirth, its stages, and challenges. We prepared ourselves to take part in the process through breathing exercises and the making of pain management decisions.

Looking at where this reclaiming of the birth process has taken us now a half century later, taboo and secrecy are gone, support is the watchword, expectant parents make a birthing plan. Births may be accompanied by a midwife or birthing doula. The coming into life can happen at home, in a birthing center, or in a section of a hospital where all that's needed for the birth is available. And family, friends, and other children can be near at hand.

As for the dying process, advances in medical science for end-of-life care, palliative care, and hospice means that what people fear most (suffering in pain) does not have to happen. But getting to that point requires what was done in the birthing process: learning about the process of dying, its stages, its challenges, and making a plan. Called an advance directive, it instructs medical personnel as to what procedures you do or do not wish performed once there is little-to-no chance of your recovery.

Support is also necessary. You need to appoint an advocate to speak on your behalf if you are unable to speak for yourself. This person becomes your Medical Power of Attorney to ensure that expensive unnecessary scans, tests, and painful procedures won't interfere with your peaceful and pain-free transition. Like birthing, dying can be returned to the home, if desired, or to a section of a hospital where all that is needed for the dying process is available. Death doulas can offer support, and family and friends can be nearby.

Awareness, knowledge, and acceptance of the going out of life process still has quite a way to go to match the progress made by the birthing process. But just as women who experienced this new approach demanded more say in it and shared with others the joy and light they found, those of us who have had the experience of accompanying and companioning a loved one through their dying process need to share the experiences of the light, the joy, and the wisdom that Socrates predicted we would find there.

Death, Dying, and the Ultimate Reality

Once we overcome the taboo and stop ignoring death, and we face and learn something of the dying process, we are confronted with Ultimate Reality—a force and power that transcends all other realties, outside the domain of time and space. In our multi-religious, multi-ethnic culture, this force has many names: God, First Mother/Heavenly Father, Tao, Creator, Consciousness, Universe, Energy, Love, Great Spirit, Life Force. These names relate to the religious and spiritual traditions or scientific principles behind them. Perhaps they can be summed up in the Native American salutation, "Great Mystery, Great All That Is!"

Some people have strong faith and certainty about what that other world looks like, others say it is unknowable. Some pray *for* the deceased, others pray *to* them, and some engage in both practices. Most would agree, there is more to life than the time an individual is alive in their body on this earth. Whatever awaits us on the other side must be, in its vastness and complexity a mystery. I remember finding a pamphlet in the back of the church when I was in elementary school with a title I've never forgotten: *Your God is Too Small*.

Artists and Ultimate Reality

"Sing in me, Muse, and through me, tell the story," the ancient poets prayed. To this day, many artists will tell you that their inspiration and creativity seem to come from something outside of themselves, out of their ordinary state of consciousness. The classical meaning of the term "muse" comes from Greek mythology, where nine goddesses were considered the source of the knowledge embodied in poetry and lyric songs. Art history confirms the strong connection that the arts and creativity had with goddesses, the ancient's version of Ultimate Reality. The Egyptian goddess Hathor represented the musical arts and dance. The Hindu goddess of creativity, Maa Saraswathi, who was credited with inventing the Sanskrit language, was assigned music, art, and wisdom. It was said that her rays dispelled the darkness of ignorance. The Celtic goddess, Brit, in addition to poetic arts and crafts, was thought to carry and dispense the gifts of prophecy and divination to her worshippers.

The artist Frida Kahlo maintained, "I am my own muse. I am the subject I know best. The subject I want to know better." In using the arts to grieve, art-making becomes the path to such future self-knowledge and to an increased connection with the Ultimate Reality that could be thought of as ones' own muse.

In companioning people that are experiencing the death of a loved one, it can be important to have a rudimentary understanding of the Ultimate Reality that carries meaning for them. Visual artists made a major contribution to this task through the artistic visual symbols they offer. The Jewish six-pointed star of David, the Christian cross, the Catholic crucifix, the star and crescent of Islam, the yin and yang circle of Taoism, the wheel of Buddhism, and the calligraphy letters of Hinduism express what cannot be expressed in words alone. When the images are placed in a circle together around the universal peace symbol or a heart symbol, they serve as bridges between consciousness, the world, and the sacred.

Photography: Life Before Death

Several years ago, on a vacation trip to Montreal, I encountered a photography exhibition in a gallery at the Notre Dame Cathedral with the intriguing title "Life Before Death." It reminded me of a tribute a friend made to his father. "My father was a courageous man. Unlike the cowards who die a thousand deaths, he lived his life fully each day, and only at the end of his life did he die." Though some might consider this a strange subject to pursue while on vacation, I couldn't resist seeing how the arts of photography and storytelling might enhance our understanding of death and dying.

German photographer Walter Schels and journalist Beate Lakotta admit to beginning the project to alleviate their own fear and discomfort with the subject of dying. Visiting their work, I see how they have most likely accomplished that goal for many others as well. The artists got permission to photograph twenty-four people who were living in hospices in Hamburg and Berlin. Subjects were photographed once during the initial interview and then again shortly after their death.

The exhibit featured two gigantic versions of the photographs of each person, displayed side by side, along with their stories. Included in the mix were some who had been vital and alive only a few months before, then stricken suddenly with something like an inoperable brain tumor. One pairing, that of a six-year-old boy whose two pictures were placed next to the pictures of his mother, stood out for me. Both were suffering with the same terminal disease. The mother's story told of her prayer to stay alive long enough for her son to go before her. That prayer was answered, but not the next prayer to stay around long enough to raise the boy's twin. She died less than a month after her afflicted son.

Some people depicted seemed to thrive in the environment of the hospice facility. One man lived a good year longer than anyone had expected, dying shortly after he had been notified that he would have to leave the facility. This resonated with me since I knew two women whose mothers had been thrown out of hospice services twice for no longer meeting the criteria.

Some people expressed regret that their life was ending since they felt it was just beginning. Having worked all their lives, they were looking forward to enjoying retirement or a new relationship. Several men who had lived for their work, without attachments to family and friends, expressed the feeling that they had not lived.

One death that felt especially blessed to me was of a man whose wife spent every one of his last days with him. She described having a kind of intimacy that hadn't been available to them in other circumstances in their lives. Another woman in her sixties told a moving story of forgiveness and reconciliation. She had gone through a contemptuous divorce many years prior and hadn't spoken to her former husband for seventeen years. When she entered hospice, she decided to call and ask him to come and be with her at her deathbed. He did so and it seemed to allow her to die peacefully. All the stories provided lessons, but some demonstrated there is much life still in the process of dying.

I used to know my name.
Now I don't.
I think a river understands me,
for what does it call itself
in that blessed moment when
it starts emptying into the infinite
luminous sea?

-Hafiz

Between the Worlds

Not only do we not "practice dying," but most people in Western culture know very little about the process of dying and how to be with someone when death is transpiring. Of course, not all deaths can be accompanied. Many happen suddenly and without warning from an accident or a person dies unexpectedly in their sleep or from a stroke or heart attack. The dying process then can be nearly instantaneous.

As my beloved eighty-three-year-old Auntie started across the room, she was making a joke about the piano-playing pitcher for the Tigers who had just won the pennant. Before she got to the other side of the room, she collapsed and was dead before her body reached the floor. The gift was that that she did not have to deal with serious disabilities or lingering procedures before she died. For her loved ones, we were left in shock, remembering, and replaying our last conversations with her. But for those dying of diseases, like some types of cancer, it can be a gift to be able to comfort and be comforted, to express appreciations, to say goodbye, and to live close to whatever you call the Ultimate Reality—in the liminal space and time referred to as "between the worlds."

It's been nearly thirty years since my friend Rose called from a hospital in Nebraska to say that "the cancer had spread everywhere" and that she was dying. Later, she extended an invitation. "Come and be with me while I do this, and then I will be with you when it's your turn." *How could that work?* I thought, but I didn't say that. I flew to Nebraska from Texas, but not before calling my Women's Spirituality teacher and friend Glenda Taylor to engage her as my backup coach. I didn't know much, but I knew I needed support for this caregiving/health advocate role.

In those days before you could Google your questions,

we didn't know about the timing of the dying process. On the fourth or fifth day we were together, Rose said, "This seems to be taking longer than I thought it would. How does it seem to you?" I agreed with her perception, but I thought it might be like when life is coming in. My delivery nurse used to say, "No matter what the calendar or the numbers say, babies come when they're ready to come."

There is a limit to how long one can remain pregnant and there are limits and stages to the dying process as well. Medical experts say that for the three weeks or so of the pre-active dying phase, a person usually detaches from social activities and spends more time sleeping. This was true to some extent, but when Rose and I were together in her hospital room, or when my son Ken lay in the high-ceilinged living room of our home we'd turned into the dying room, and for our daughter Corinne, when her hospital bed occupied the den of her family's home, there was a lot of life-affirming social activity and insightful conversations.

Things got done. Before Rose went to the hospital, as chair of the Nebraska Commission on Women, she had been leading an effort to plan an upcoming state-wide women's healthcare conference. So, the women visiting her hospital room picked up where she'd left off, and together they finished the planning. Ken experienced reunions with theater friends and celebrated his thirty-first birthday with a party that included dancing and singing in his hospital room. His hairdresser friend, Les, brought his supplies and taught Ken's stepdad, Rich, how to shave his head.

Corinne woke from a dream with the answer to a dilemma her husband's family had been dealing with for years regarding his quite elderly grandmother. Her determination and clarity got the wheels turning to move Gam to a high-end assisted living facility. She didn't want to go, but after seeing

135

the place, I called and told her, "You are gonna love it! You will think you're in Heaven and you didn't have to die to get there."

Some people refer to the Ultimate Reality as energy, and the energy in those spaces was palpable. One woman delivering flowers commented, "It's hard to leave this space. There is so much love here." I suspect that this had to do with what my mentor Glenda refers to as "going into ceremonial time," a time when past, present, and future can be perceived simultaneously.

During the active stage of dying, which is generally thought to last three days, many things can influence the person's readiness and ability to let go. "A major organ must fail for death to occur," we were told when Kenneth was dying. For young people, their organs are often in pretty good shape, despite whatever it is that is causing their death.

Thirty to forty-five percent of people experience a period of agitation during the dying process, and this is when the arts of music, video, audiobooks, and singing can be helpful to patients and their family members. At one point, Rose had trouble relaxing enough to go to sleep, so we secured a video of nature scenes set to music which played on a loop and helped her get through that rough patch.

Ken played songs from his collection of Broadway shows, and I still remember the lines of reassurance from *The Sound of Music* that filled the room as my blue latex-gloved hands massaged Ken's sore leg.

> "...*For here you are, standing there, loving me,*
> *whether or not you should.*
> *So somewhere in my youth or childhood,*
> *I must have done something good.*"

The timing of the person's letting go can be affected by many things, including who has arrived and who is still in transit. Rose waited for her daughter Jill's visit, which got postponed a couple of times. When my daughter Corinne seemed to be hanging on longer than humanly possible given the numbers on the equipment attached to her, I feared she might be holding on for her father to arrive from Oregon. When I learned that he wasn't coming, I did what hospice team members suggest and I told her that it was okay for her to leave and that I would say goodbye to him for her. Ken left only a few minutes after my sister had arrived just after midnight. That timing meant that I had support as he transitioned.

When Corinne's husband called me back into the room just as her spirit was leaving her body, I had a vision of streaming strings of light breaking their bonds with her body. I thought if those strings were attached to all the people who wanted her to stay, no wonder it took her so long to leave.

Hearing is the last of the senses to go, so music and song are valuable accompaniments to a person's dying journey. A woman told me of the last hours of her mother's life. She no longer had language, but she was a jazz aficionado, and as she lay peacefully on her death bed, her big toe tapped in perfect timing to the rhythm of the jazz music her son played for her.

Volunteer threshold choirs sing for people who are on that threshold between life and death, perhaps an example of what Ram Dass calls "singing one another home." But I had never heard of this practice when I took Rose's hand and sang to her one of the songs from Glenda's spirituality group. I was singing, "You are woman, you grow **out** of the earth," but on the second verse, the words switched for me and became, "You are woman you, **go back** to the earth," and at that moment, after fourteen days of trying to die, Rose left.

Celebrating Births

The ritual of celebrating the day someone is born is not universal in all cultures, but in mine, it's consistent. It starts early, posing an icing-covered toddler in his highchair for his first official birthday portrait. Next come the bounce house backyard parties for young school-aged children, or the trays of birthday cupcakes their parents deliver to their school classrooms, though I've heard some schools have stopped allowing that. After kids can reach the kitchen counter, they turn the tables on their parents, cooking them a birthday breakfast, totally devastating the kitchen, then serving it to them in bed.

Folks of all ages congratulate one another on social media with colorful emojis and symbols of good wishes on their special day. If you're shy, you might want to decline the luncheon invitation to avoid the restaurant servers collecting around your table to sing a chorus of "Happy Birthday" while people you don't know gawk at you or join in. Far-flung families call one another and leave sung voicemail messages while workplaces gather everyone in the breakroom to celebrate the employees whose birthday will fall in the present month. And we can't leave out the "today's the birthday of…" signs in the bannered dining rooms of senior care centers. The balloons, the cards, the candles, the songs—all ritual items to help us exclaim in family and community, "We're glad you were born and happy that you made it for another year."

Birthdays might be a good time to acknowledge that getting to an actual day of birth is not the most common outcome for a fertilized egg. Many miscarry, or spontaneously abort, often before a woman is even aware that she is pregnant. Our ancestors who lived close to the land stayed aware of this. Working in my garden, as the seeds are scattered by the wind,

I know that only a small number of them will find success in becoming a living replication of their parent plant.

This awareness is most likely the reason couples hesitate to announce their pregnancy to friends and family members in the early months—not wanting to set themselves up for deep feelings of communal grief and loss. As my own mother and daughter each learned through their own personal experiences, a natural abortion is relatively common, especially in the early months, and especially if it is a woman's first pregnancy.

These scientific facts and the experiences of friends and family throughout the years increase my desire to celebrate birthdays, my own and others, and particularly the birthdays of those who have gone from us. Part of grieving well is maintaining a relationship with a deceased loved one, remembering the gift to our life that they have been. The practice of remembering and honoring each of my children on the anniversary of the day I birthed them keeps a strong connection to them and to the gratitude I have for the gift their lives have been to mine.

The rarity of birth days and the joy we receive remembering our deceased or living children's birthdays fuels my passion to change the way we relate to bereaved parents who have lost infants. Since these loved ones did not live long enough to become known to many others, the parents of miscarried children or those who died in infancy are left alone to suffer in silence and pressured to forget and move on. But for many parents, this is not desired or even possible.

My dancing social worker friend Lynn Coghill lost one of her twin sons shortly after his birth twenty-some years ago. When she returned from the hospital with only one son, she had to hold grief in one side of her heart and gratitude in the other. This continued as she took care of and raised her living son. "The fact that my two sons have the same birthday is a kind of blessing. I remember Christopher as I'm celebrating Matt's birthday." Their shared birthdays give Lynn the opportunity to never forget and continue to love both sons she gave birth to.

Even if it is not the practice in your family or culture to celebrate the day you were born, find a day to celebrate that birthday, and that occasion of those who have gone from your sight, in whatever way you can. This then becomes a way to increase your gratitude for the gift of life itself. As the mystery writer Agatha Christie puts it, "I have sometimes been wildly, desperately, acutely miserable, racked with sorrow, but though it all, I still know quite certainly that just to be alive is a grand thing."

Funerals and Celebrations of Life

Funerals are ceremonies often held in religious settings, like churches or in funeral homes, shortly after a person's death and preceding their burial. Memorials or celebrations of life can occur at any time after a person's death and in a variety of settings, including online. In all instances, they are reminders of our own inevitable demise. "Don't ask for whom the bell tolls, it tolls for thee." Such awareness correlates to increased appreciation and gratitude for whatever time we, the living, have left. We don't get to know how a life turns out until it ends, so details brought to life at an elder's memorial can provide inspiration and encouragement to those left behind.

Like most people, I have been at the funeral of someone whose life ended before they had the opportunity to live it fully. The stories of a whole life are too big for individual bodies to hold. Various people offer aspects of a person not known to others. Being present for those personal story snippets provides a fuller picture of the deceased person and their life.

There is no substitute for people showing up in person, no better comfort than the presence of real people taking time out of their busy schedules to create a communal container to hold the pain and tragedy experienced by those left behind. As we sit in silence together, or meditate or pray or sing, or stand in line to offer condolences, or cry or dabble at our tears or those of another, or shake hands or hug the mourners, or recount our recollections of the deceased, we become one as witnesses. We became companions, part of an energy field not commonly found at other gatherings. Its name is LOVE.

A Destination Memorial

It's a rainy Saturday afternoon in Newport, Oregon and the comfortable modern lobby of the Holiday Inn Express is uncharacteristically busy. The printer/copy machine has been in continual operation for a while as three twenty-something young people, and what appears to be their father, an uncle, their grandmother, and cousin, a younger maybe ten-year-old girl, are collaborating on an upcoming event.

"We found these jazz albums in his record collection," someone says, "so we need Ella Fitzgerald and Duke Ellington." Someone else remembers, "How about Coltrane? What's his first name?" The attractive woman in sweats and a long blonde braid seems to be in charge of the music, telling everyone, "Just get me the exact title of the song or piece you want, and I'll find it on Spotify."

The tall, slender young man appears to be editing a document as the group decides to divide it into four segments so each grandchild can read a section. "Has anyone timed the reading of this whole thing?" somebody asks.

This must be the way it looked to the hotel desk clerk, who asked me the following morning, "Were you preparing for a memorial?" Yes, I said, "You've heard of destination weddings? Well, for our far-flung family, this is a destination funeral ritual. We've flown here from five different states to celebrate the life of our eldest member who lived here the last twenty years of his ninety-four-year-long life. He died five months ago. She didn't ask, but the look on her face seemed to say, "Wow! Why would you go to so much trouble?"

To answer that question, even to myself, I look to what grief expert Alan D. Wolfelt calls The Six Reconciliation Needs of Mourning:

1. Acknowledging the reality of the death.

When my father took me into the front parlor of his aunt's home in rural Illinois to view her dead body lying in a casket there, the reality of her death was confirmed, if a bit scary to my young mind. In more recent times, church funerals and visitations help those who mourn to confront the reality of their loss. Mary Frances O'Connor's recent research and book *The Grieving Brain* confirms the fact that, even though we have been told of someone's death, the brain holds on to the notion that the loved one is merely absent from our life presently and likely to return. When the deceased person lives far away, and our contact with them is infrequent, the need for a ritual of confirmation of their death is enhanced.

2. Move toward the pain of the loss.

Healthy grieving requires communal support to feel and express our sorrow — an occasion and a ritual space. It was my grandchildren's idea to fly across the country and meet in person, invite the local people, to thank them personally for standing in for us, and supporting their grandfather in his last years. And to add to the degree of difficulty, to do a simultaneous online Zoom of the event for friends and family across the country who couldn't make the trip. Though this hybrid version of a celebration of a life was complex and difficult to pull off, it still would meet my mentor Anna Halprin's definition that "ritual is love made visible," and a reminder that love is the core of what still survives and never dies.

3. Remember the person who died.

In the ritual space, and afterwards, the arts of storytelling, music, song, and photo images encourage recalling and remembering the deceased loved one and the part their life stories played in our individual lives. As to the biography the grandchildren put together and read, I'm not sure how many people contributed to it or who ended up doing the final edits, but it was a comprehensive document of events and influences through the years that connected us to our pain and provided solace for it.

4. Develop a new self-identity.

We each know a specific version of a person, depending on our relationship to them. George's supervisor at the lighthouse, where George had written a book about its history and supervised its renovation, told some endearing stories that highlighted George's determination to *do the right thing*, no matter what it took to accomplish that.

After failing to influence the higher ups that the rocks someone dumped around the base of the lighthouse were causing water to seep in and threatened its survival, he wrote a letter to the editor of the local paper about the matter. When that didn't change anything, he contacted his congressional representative, and, although the lighthouse was not a federal property, the rocks were removed, and the danger eliminated. "Everyone saw him as 'The Keeper,' he just made himself that. He's lucky he wasn't an employee, or he'd have been fired," the gentleman said with a laugh. Later, George's son said, "You know, I never saw much similarity between myself and my father, but when I heard that story, I thought, 'That's me. I do that.'"

5. Search for meaning.

As George's former spouse, I decided to highlight for our grandchildren some of the events of his life that I'd been present for as examples of values and practices that I would like to see them continue in their own lives. They laughed when I mentioned there were plenty of things to avoid and not continue, but they probably already knew what those were, so no need to dwell on them.

"The three things I would wish you to continue in your own lives are:

a) As a news broadcaster, George focused on what he knew to be important from the perspective of history and *he was guided, not by uninformed opinion, but by what he knew to be true*. This practice could guide us all through what's been a rough patch of disinformation in our public

144

discourse of late.

b) We are all products of the times in which we live, and George's time and experience happened during the quest for civil and voting rights for Black people in our country. As a radio disk jockey while still in high school, he featured and admired the innovators of jazz music, most of whom were African Americans. This, and his love of the improvisational art form of jazz, gave him an 'out of the box' way of thinking, and this quest for justice became personal to him. He was known for being what we would call today "an active ally" for this movement. My wish for our grandchildren is that, during your time here, you become involved in whatever issue you feel would make the earth a better place for its inhabitants. Rather than being a bystander, become a part of the making of history as he was.

c) To George, love was an action word, which meant doing what you love and sharing it with others. It meant stopping at the lighthouse to see if they had some plans that he could copy to make a miniature wooden lighthouse for his grandsons. Then staying to become its keeper. May you find and do what you love and share it.

6. Receive ongoing support from others.

Something we learned during Covid—when they were taken away from us—we need funerals, memorials, and rituals to celebrate and appreciate what we have loved and lost. We need memories to sustain us as we build enduring connections to those who have gone before us, and perhaps to live out their legacy in our own lives. My ten-year-old granddaughter, Kyra, told a story of a gift her grandfather had given her. "I just loved the fake toy telephone that Grandpa George gave me when I was six. It made me so happy, and it made him happy that I loved it so much." Taking a breath and a pause she said, "I guess the lesson we can take from his life is that even the small things can be really important."

Teaching Children the Art of Grieving

Our legacies become what we contribute to the next generation, and teaching children the art of grieving could be considered a worthwhile gift to pass on. The first experience young children have with grief and loss is likely to be the death of a pet. Parents' common first impulse is to try and protect their children from the feelings that a loss naturally engenders: sadness, grief, anguish, and perhaps anger. Our culture has made grave errors in attempting to protect children by not including them in funerals or by restricting them from the bedside of a dying loved one, or trying to spare them the truth that someone they love is likely to die soon. As I saw with many therapy clients, the negative effect of these "protective" measures can rob the young person of the opportunity to observe and develop lifelong skills to effectively cope with loss.

Walking my dog one morning last summer, I stumbled onto an example of how some parents of young children in my neighborhood had clearly made the most of the teaching moment when their child lost a pet. Cody started to pull the leash, and I could see he was drawn to something underneath one of the bushes that line a communal driveway in our neighborhood. Looking closely at the spot, I identified an arrangement of a small rock and a feather, and moving closer, realized that someone had purposefully placed these items to mark this particular spot.

Reading the inscription on the rock, I learned that Cody and I had stumbled onto a now sacred space—the gravesite of a child's pet. I imagined the ceremony that likely took place there as the child and their parents carried their loved one in a formal procession from their home to this resting place. As the note on the rock detailed, "On Dec. 23rd, we remember Creamer and the wonderful joy he gave to our family—the best fish in the whole world!"

Communal ritual is one of the most time-honored methods of grieving and companioning others through their grief. And this family had illustrated for the young people in their lives one of the most prominent gifts of grieving: the gratitude it opens in our hearts for the life of the loved one— person or pet—and for the time we had with them.

Artist Resource

1. Take a look at my favorite birthday song, taught to me by some African-American women friends, "God danced the day you were born, the angels did the bump to Gabriel's horn, God danced the day you were born, grateful for the gift of you."

2. For the most transformational experience of joy amidst the deepest sorrow, see the video, *My Joy is Heavy!* by The Bengsons.

3. From the time when one of the members of our improv troupe was in the place between the worlds and we danced in person beside his bed, we've had on our playlist the song *Lift Me Up* written by hospice chaplain Jesse Palidofsky from his album *Dancing Toward the Light.* So, in hearing that one

of the longtime leaders of InterPlay had entered hospice, we organized an online recording of thirty or so people dancing to this song on his behalf. We sent the recording to him and his wife as a love note to reverberate across the miles. We highly recommend it if you'd like to try it in your community. Here are some of the lyrics:

"Wandering in this wilderness/ lost without a guide/ just an ordinary man/ trying to make it to the other side. Don't treat me like a leper/ Ease my weary load/ A simple human touch/ and I will feel less alone."

Reflection/Action

1. Write your own obituary and ask family members to write theirs. Then trade them and discuss what's important to each of you about your legacy, how you want to be remembered.

2. Imagine your own "time between the worlds," if you should be able to have one. Where would you like it to be, who would you like to be with you, and what music, videos, poems, or other art forms would you like to have in the space? Then write it down and/or share this with someone.
3. Make sure you have an advance directive and a health advocate assigned in writing, and let people know where this paperwork can be found.

4. Share with family members and friends what you would like to happen at your memorial or funeral.

Part III
Implementation: How the Arts Help Us Grieve

"Life imitates art more than art imitates life."

-Oscar Wilde

Chapter Nine

Storytelling: Making Meaning and Sharing Truth

During the time of our daughter's journey with breast cancer, through the months that melted into years of diagnoses, treatments, X-rays, scans, blood tests and drug trials, and the rollercoaster of treatment successes and failures, my husband and I were cautious in talking with one another about our personal feelings and reactions. As mental health professionals, we were aware of the statistics that eighty percent of marriages do not survive the death of a child. Our relationship had survived the death of our son, but we knew our grieving styles were very different (which is quite common for men and women in Western culture), as were our family roles.

I was, at times, our daughter's caregiver, at other times, the grandmother, taking care of my three grandchildren. Both my roles were up close and personal while Rich continued to work, pay bills, and negotiate practical matters involved in supporting our daughter and her family. Fortunately, we each had friends who companioned us when our individual emotional plates were full. I relied on close women friends from my work and members of my women's spirituality group.

Rich had several male friends that called themselves "the cave buds" who offered support through the distraction of playing golf and putting energy into work projects.

We came together during InterPlay storytelling sessions. These communities, in various parts of the world, provided us with what every grief-stricken mourner needs: fair witnessing, listeners to our telling. One of the forms, Side-by-Side Stories, invites two people to stay in their own version of an agreed upon topic and to talk about it while allowing more than the usual amount of space in between sentences and phrases. Like the way that music encourages instrumental themes to overlap one another or blend and contrast, the audience is hearing both speakers. They have an active role in alternating their attention between the two voices, the two versions of the story. The performers are not listening to one another, their focus is on their own story, but sometimes they will catch a phrase or a word from the other person and are encouraged to include the phrase in their story. (For example, if a fire engine siren happens during the storytelling, the improvisational storyteller might find a way to include that in their own telling.)

One storytelling occasion, when we were coming near the time to end (and that's part of the side-by-side storytelling task, to find an ending together), I heard my husband say, "We did everything we could…" and I repeated what I heard him say, putting it in my own story, "We did everything we could…" and then we said together, "We did everything we could, and nothing worked."

Silence blanketed the room. The InterPlay improvisational form we used, and the container created by witnesses and storytellers, allowed us all to recognize and accept in that moment the awful truth. A truth we have avoided saying out loud.

A year or two ago, I spoke with a woman who was in the audience on that occasion, and she still remembers it—that heightened moment of honorable surrender to the futility of all our earthly efforts. That transition to an acknowledgement of powerlessness that grievers must eventually make.

As I reflect on this now, from the perspective of nearly twenty years, I remember that Corinne had a different perspective on moments like these than I did. During times of bad news, when the treatments were not working, I would conclude that our prayers and those of all the people praying for her were not being answered. Corinne would tell me, "All prayers are answered. But sometimes the answer is 'no.'" *The task then for the griever is to take that "no" as the answer.*

Stories Remembered

Everybody loves a good story. If you were lucky enough to have a grandmother or loving aunts, you probably never tired of their repeated stories of you as a child. My aunts often told me the story of sending me to a neighborhood store for peaches. According to them, when I left, I was marching in step to a repeating chant, "Peaches, peaches, peaches." They suspected something may have gone wrong when I came back marching in step to the chant, "Pears, pears, pears." And yes, though I only know this from their report, I did buy pears. So, stories can be how we learn about and stay in touch with our younger selves.

Stories people tell us of our loved ones give us a background for knowing them better. I learned a lot about the complexity and dysfunction of my grandparents' households through the often-told story of my mother and her sister walking to school together every day, asking each other, "Are we sure we're really sisters? We don't live in the same house."

When people die, it is the stories others tell that bring them close to us and give us a broader and deeper understanding of them. Each year, as we traverse the grief spiral, we come back to the season of our loss. What we have learned from the stories and our reflection on them has changed us, providing a new perspective. Some people report feeling closer to their loved one since their death. Some notice that their loved one has more influence in their lives now in unexpected ways. The stories we tell ourselves have changed so that we see our loved one more clearly from this greater distance. What we once found annoying may have softened. What seemed heroic or saintly may now have leveled out to become an appreciation for the courage of their ordinary humanity.

We're wired for story. From the time we were drawing spirals on cave walls, attempting to survive together in a dangerous world, till now, when marketers use stories to sell us their products, the structure of storytelling has taught us what is important to pay attention to. It is said that the shortest distance between two people is a story, so stories are what connect us. Being wired for narrative, whether written or spoken, listened to, or read, we learn from other people's experiences, from their accounts of what they've found worth paying attention to, and what conclusions they've drawn. Paying attention to our own stories, even playing with the way we tell them, is how we process our own life experiences, learn what we think about something, grieve our losses, and become more of who we truly are.

Writing Our Own Stories

According to one of my writing mentors, Elizabeth Jarett Andrews, "Writers famously write to find out what we think." She finds that, "In my private moments there's space to pull something new into the world. At the writing desk, I make... as it turns out, my life." Looking back on my own grieving process these past twenty years, I would say that learning to create and recreate stories of my loss experiences—written, sometimes edited and reviewed, at other times, momentarily spoken and crafted in the moment in the presence of respectful witnesses—is an important way that I have processed and metabolized my grief. It's how I have come to understand that the cycle of grieving and the growth it brings forth are how we create a satisfying life, and how we create a place for the new version of ourselves in it.

Journaling

Forms of journaling or writing for oneself on a regular basis is a common practice begun by some of us soon after we learned to write. In 1972, the artist and playwright Julia Cameron published the book *The Artist's Way*, promoting a daily ritual she named "The Morning Pages." These are three pages of longhand stream of consciousness writing done first thing in the morning. No preplanning, no editing, no sharing with others. The practice is said to clear one's mind, to build self-confidence, and create a path for greater creativity.

Since much of what we write, if it's to clear our mind or express our feelings, is likely rooted in grief and loss. I might suggest a version titled with a slightly different spelling,

The Mourning Pages. You might want to look at what you've written to help you process the losses that come to mind and appreciate the surprise alchemy that may likely occur there.

If you are one of those people who has continued some version of journaling, of putting your feelings onto a page into and through adulthood, psychologists would predict that you are physically healthier than people who do not engage in this practice.

The strong link between expressive writing and physical health has been scientifically documented beginning in 1982 by psychologist James Pennebaker. College student subjects were asked to write for fifteen minutes a day for four days about any traumatic experiences they had while growing up that they hadn't shared with anyone. The control group of students was directed to write for the same amount of time about superficial topics. Those who wrote about their trauma experiences had significantly fewer visits to the health center and fewer physical symptoms in the following year than the control group.

During the pandemic, writer Suleika Jaquad started an online community of people supporting one another to continue writing for themselves. The writers were offered, if they chose, to share their writings during the lockdown. Suleika, who had been separated from her usual life due to undergoing a bone marrow transplant, named her site *The Isolation Journal* and it quickly grew to over 100,000 participants. Her description of journal writing fits with how I define using the arts to process grief. "I make of this writing a ritual to mark the thresholds, to traverse the valleys and the peaks, to honor the space between the no longer and the not yet."

Ritual Containers

In early grief, most people look to family and friends for a listening ear as they process their losses. As Rose said, "I don't know what I think until I hear myself say it." If the person is fortunate, such support is offered and provided. But after the flowers have wilted and the casserole dishes have been washed and returned to their senders, everyone returns to the new normal of their everyday lives. For most mourners, there is still a strong need for the attention and support of empathetic listeners. Brené Brown writes, "If we want to find the way back to ourselves and one another, we need language and the grounded confidence to both tell our stories and be stewards of the stories that we hear. This is the framework for meaningful connection." In our individualistic culture, we may not realize that what we are needing is something our ancestors took for granted—a ritual container to hold our individual and collective sorrows.

Recently, while attending the women's circle I've been a member of for over thirty years, I got some clarity on why one person or a series of individual people's good wishes or words of wisdom as we grieve are not enough. As we met, some of us for the first time in person since the pandemic, we went into circle and spoke into its center. As we told the stories of our longings, our hopes and dreams, our pain and sorrows, we were held and honored. I recognized that much of what we brought into circle were our losses of health or abilities, or those of our loved ones since the last time we'd gathered, and the container held them. We call our actions in creating this container, "going into ceremony," and our actions in speaking the details of our lives, "placing them on the altar." Whatever we call it, our grief needs a community container and the agreements and forms that hold, respect, and honor it.

Many types of groups have such an agreement and practice it by using some version of the Native American talking stick ritual. Often an art object itself, the stick is passed around the circle and each person given an opportunity to speak their truth. When you have the stick, you can talk (or pass it to the next person without speaking if you so choose.) When you don't have the stick, you listen. And since everyone has separated themselves from the responsibilities and noisy distractions of modern life (cell phones are off), there is nothing one must do. There is just being. The being together creates the group body, which seems to have an intelligence of its own.

The Quakers have a practice they use to create a ritual container during worship—one that we often borrowed to use in our clinic staff meetings. On occasions when we were faced with a difficult situation that required a decision or action, we gathered and sat in silence in our group room, going into what the Quakers call "gathered stillness." Sitting together in common purpose, we waited, listening for inspiration from what Quakers call "the Spirit of God" or the "Light Within," or from what I call, "the part of us that's smarter than we are." Though I still cannot explain how it works, I can say that it does.

Sometimes an answer would come during a session at the staff meeting or at the women's retreat. Sometimes there would be a delay. There have been occasions when one of the women would have a dream that related to either the group questions or an individual member's expressed dilemmas. One woman, when attempting to describe our group said, "We're so close, we even dream for one another." I think as neuroscientists learn more about how a single brain works, they will be able to explain what happens when we engage more brains and achieve the power of simultaneous focus.

I had such an experience of simultaneous focus when the

team of friends and advisors were helping me come up with the title of my first book. When we went into the silence together, I had no openness to changing the working title. I liked the one we already had. But sitting in that space in stillness together, when someone said the word, "Stillpoint," my whole body reverberated to let me know that that was the title.

Another structure that creates a ritual container is one used during the twelve step meetings of Alcoholics Anonymous and Al-Anon, held all over the world for nearly ninety years. Meetings begin with a reading of *Twelve Steps and Twelve Traditions,* reminding group members of their shared purpose. A chairperson helps maintain the agreement of no crosstalk or commenting when a person speaks in the meeting. As the speaker shares their challenges and grief, they are also encouraged to share their discoveries of strength and hope while dealing with diseases of addiction in themselves and/or family members. Group members support by listening and learning, and often tell a speaker after the meeting what they have gained from their sharing.

In the improvisational practice of InterPlay, storytelling forms are structured to prevent the dangers inherent in the telling and retelling of our own stories. To avoid reinfecting ourselves with the pain of the past, we vary the way the story is told, telling it in a made-up language or using only movement and gesture without any words. To avoid taking on the pain of others as they tell of their difficulties, witnesses practice going into stillness, noticing and, when asked, sharing the effect the story has had in their own bodies. "I found myself holding my breath," or, "I felt moved by your voice."

These containers and structures help us to avoid mistakes of trying to "fix" or "cheer up" the speaker, which are considered forms of disrespecting a person's grief. By participating in a respectful listening group, members can engage in actions grief educator and director of the Center for Loss and Life Transition, Alan D Wolfelt, calls true companioning, which is "listening with the heart, not analyzing with the head... being present to another person's pain; not taking it away... going to the wilderness of the soul." And most importantly, "Not thinking you are responsible for finding the way out." Mourners in these compassionate spaces are free to explore their own stories and come to their own conclusions about them.

As a therapist, I've listened to many stories and come to understand how telling a story, especially about a traumatic experience, can on some occasions heal the trauma. I believe the same is true for healing traumatic grief. We say in InterPlay that "repetition is our friend," but when the story has elements of trauma, something new must be introduced. Otherwise, like old vinyl records on a turntable, the groove deepens and the trauma and wound of the story reinfects rather than transforms. I can demonstrate this better if I take you to the Texas prison where I taught an Exploring Creativity workshop to women confined there.

We are in a gymnasium type room with about a dozen women using InterPlay forms of movement and storytelling. The form was known at the time as the Magic Spot with a Three-Sentence Story. The game begins by establishing a place that will be known as the "magic spot," and a subject or topic is introduced that everyone will say three sentences about when they take their turn standing in that spot.

One person starts a repetitive movement, and everyone follows, copying that movement until someone in the group steps onto the magic spot. The music and all the players stop, and that person says their three sentences about the agreed upon subject. The speaker then changes the repetitive movement, allowing the movement to grow out of what they have just said, and everyone follows that new movement until another person steps on the spot and says their three sentences, then changes the movement again. On this occasion, the word was "rain."

The game went on for a few minutes with one woman telling about how frizzy her hair gets when it rains, another took her turn describing how she loves sitting on a covered porch during a rainstorm, staying dry while watching and listening to the rain. Another mentioned how the dog she had as a child was always frightened by thunder.

Then a woman steps in the spot and begins her story with, "The worst beating I ever got was when I was dressed for church in a bright yellow dress, and it had rained, and there were puddles everywhere that I loved to play in." Replaying the scene, she began stomping on the floor as if there were puddles there. "I got my new Mary Jane shoes wet when I played in the puddles..." She didn't get through much more of the story because she became very emotional as she left us and went back into that time and place. She began to collapse onto the floor, and before I could get to her, the rest of the women rushed to the center of the room and surrounded her. They held her in a group hug for what seemed like a very long time.

Viewing the scene, I realized that something healing was happening for this woman in this time of telling this story. No one can ever erase the memories this woman has of being abused as a child, but now, and forever, alongside this memory, will be the memory of the response of these women—the visceral feel of their group hug.

Poetry: Words as Medicine

I'm not a poet, though I've often wished I could say profound things succinctly, to be able to express the musicality of images, highlight the rhythm of phrases and capture the tone of words. Even now, I wish I was better able to create what J. S. Mill claimed of Wordsworth's poetry: "Medicine for the mind."

As a grief advocate, I am always on the lookout for art tools that help us understand grief more deeply and grieve losses more effectively. I especially get excited when scientists and artists get together to demonstrate something that our intuition tells us is right, and that scientific processes can help explain how and why it works.

A day or so before finding this next resource, a former social work colleague, Colleen Shannon, came to my mind. Colleen was a biofeedback expert, and we worked closely together collaborating on publications, before I left the university in the late eighties. One of our collaborations was an article titled, *The Body-Mind Connection: What Social Workers Need to Know.* For years afterwards, Colleen and I met monthly over lunch, taking turns picking up the check so we would always have a reason to meet again. She died of ovarian cancer in the late nineties, so I wondered what made me think of her. Then I came across an article about poetry and biofeedback. "Pay attention here, Sheila," Colleen seemed to be telling me. The June 27, 2022 article by Marissa Grunes with videos by Steven Allardi was titled *Feeling Stressed? Read a Poem.*

The article sprang from the experience of two literary scholars, Jonathan Bate and Paula Byrne, who found nothing of interest to read, while sitting in a hospital waiting room while their five-year-old daughter was in surgery. Since they were committed to the notion that literature can heal, they decided to put together a book of poems, *Stressed, Unstressed: Classic Poems to Ease the Mind.*

Before publication, they connected with biofeedback researcher Inna Khazan to see if she could help them demonstrate that reciting poetry can affect heartrate variability and synchronize a person's breathing to lessen the stress response. For the study, the researchers selected Robert Frost's poem *Stopping by Woods on a Snowy Evening*, which the poet himself reported composing in what he called a "flow state." This concept, now confirmed by positive psychology, identifies a mental state in which a person is fully immersed in a feeling of energized focus and enjoyment. When the research subject was reading the poem, measurements on the biofeedback machine confirmed that the person reading the poem had entered the relaxed flow state as well.

When I think of a poem that has taught me much about grief, I think about working with a group of nuns to help them celebrate the 150th anniversary of their community's time in America. It became clear as we reviewed their history that their successes were made possible by the way they confronted tough challenges and grieved multiple losses throughout the generations. We looked for a way to express the gifts their grief had brought them when one sister suggested the poem *The Well of Grief* by David Whyte.

Since we were proposing to dance to the poem, another sister volunteered a couple of bolts of sheer blue and turquoise fabric that she happened to have in her storage closet. Preparing to move to the poem reminded me of a comment my friend Gail Langstroth, a tri-lingual poet and eurythmy performer, said when she saw us dance to a poem, "If we don't get up and move, we are one dead cadaver walking around with feelings blocked. We can't have good thinking. We can't be creative. Movement with meaning is the alpha and omega of all health." Here's the poem and some of what we discovered as dancers.

As we moved with the fabric and the recitation of the poem's varied phrases and pauses, we began to embody its message more fully. The first lines call attention to the people who are unwilling to grieve, who avoid going deeply into the pain of their grief.

The Well of Grief

Those who will not slip beneath
the still surface on the well of grief,
turning downward through its black water
to the place we cannot breathe,

The next lines reveal the reward of going into grief:

will never know the source from which we drink,
the secret water, cold and clear,
nor find in the darkness glimmering,
the small round coins,
thrown by those who wished for something else.

All grievers had wished for something else, but in taking that dive into darkness, unexpected treasures are illuminated, and our courage is rewarded. Dancing to this poem, and observing others dance to it, took me into the watery underworld of the well, where our breath is held. We emerge relieved, refreshed, even joyful. This was my first experience of interacting with a poem that expressed the daring assertion that grief can be a positive and enlightening experience—a gift to those willing to mourn.

When my son Ken died in the Dallas Fort Worth area, my friend Jyoti, the business manager for our clinic, was in California and could not find a flight home in time for his funeral. She sent a story poem and asked that it be read at his service.

"I once knew a boy,
a sweet, enchanted boy.
Or so the song goes.
And there was something about Kenneth
that did seem enchanted and fey;
an innocence and wonder
with a shy grin that said,
"I'm open to life and all its fickle offerings."

"I want to live," said Kenneth
when he feared he wouldn't,
and his life said the same.
Kenneth just wanted to be Kenneth.
A person who had pleasure in helping to solve
other people's problems,
and did so with uncommon grace.

I watched him once, one sunny, fine day,
taking obvious pleasure
in arranging a vase of flowers
in such a way as to be
a work of art.
And it was just a lunch, a normal lunch,
but Kenneth liked grace in his life,
and grace he would have.
When he became ill,
with as ungraceful an illness
as has ever been loosed on the earth,
he still sought a graceful existence.

He still sought for all things beautiful,
and he knew love.

We shall miss your grace,
dear Kenneth,
and your deep lessons
of loving beauty.

-Jyoti King, June 1997

Funerals and Memorials

Storytelling is a central part of many funerals and memorials, sometimes during the formal ceremony in the form of a eulogy—a speech of praise dating back to Greek poetry, later popularized by the Christian Church. Storytelling is important during the less formal parts as well, like the visitation before the service, the vigils and wakes, and the home visits of Judaism's week-long mourning period known as "sitting shiva." People's personal stories enlarge or fill in our picture of the loved one being remembered and enhance our celebration of and gratitude for our loved one's life.

As we were preparing Ken's service, I heard from his community college theater teacher who provided me with a copy of a video tape of Ken's performance as Oliver in the college production of that show. So, through the magic of technology, we were taken back in time to a twenties-something Ken singing *Consider Yourself One of the Family* at his own funeral. The best demonstration of the effect this and other versions of storytelling by his family and friends had at his memorial were comments made by some of our professional

166

colleagues. "I'm sorry I never got to meet Ken," one woman said, "but thanks to today, I feel like I got to know him."

In Western culture, the obituary is a written story, a summation of the person's life at the end, when we know how it all turned out. Newspapers used to hire skilled storytellers to interview and rewrite the obituaries of people whose lives they determined were telling a larger story that would be of interest to their readers. This happened when my father died in the Detroit area in 1999.

After someone in our family or the funeral home had submitted an obituary to the paper, a reporter called my father's home and two of my sisters were interviewed. The newspaper article that resulted from this information included a photo and carried the headline, "Joe Smith: Engineer Called Self-Made Man." After the story appeared, some cousins interrogated us on how the newspaper came to write and publish this story about him. Their tone of inquiry suggested that maybe we had paid someone off to get them to write the story. After all, he wasn't a famous person.

When I compare what I emphasized about my father and his life in the eulogy that I delivered after his mass, and the article that appeared in the Detroit Free Press, it's clear that story is shaped not just by the facts of the person's life. The storyteller's relationship to the deceased person, their experience of them, and the audience for whom it is designed and delivered is what matters.

I started my story with, "Dad was a quiet man in a noisy family," and mentioned later, "Dad was a prompt person in a family of tardy people," and, "a homebody who loved to travel." The conclusions I drew from his life came at the end, in the message I delivered directly to him.

"So, Dad, you did not want to be considered 'an old man,' which is what you told us when we tried to do things for you in Florida. But you have given the term new meaning for all the people whose lives you have touched. You have shown us how to live and how to age—how to grow as you age into the best that you can be, enjoying 'the last of life for which the first was made.' And for this, and all the gifts you gave, we thank you." The "we" I refer to is, of course, all the people in the church who knew and loved him.

These experiences of looking back on someone's life through the eyes of those who knew them has caused me to reflect on when and how do we get to really know someone, and come to know ourselves? Soren Kierkegaard is credited with saying, "Life can only be understood by looking backward, but we must live life forward," without that broader perspective.

Anne was a writer and student of mine who playfully used to refer to me as "*My* Sheila." This was a nod to what writers are perhaps more in touch with than other people, which is the notion that what she knew of me was her version of me. So, to me, she became "*My* Anne." At the end of a life, that time when we can begin to understand the person more fully, our version of a person becomes enlarged and deepened by hearing from others and the stories of their experiences with our person. Eulogies, those speeches of praise and honor at a memorial, are important ways this magic occurs. So, when the funeral director, in a meeting regarding my sister Mary Jane's memorial, stated to my two nieces and remaining sister that "we don't eulogize," I was shocked.

Though I had no idea who the "we" referred to, as the matriarch of the family, I had to protest. "Here's the problem," I said. "We are Irish. We're storytellers, and Mary Jane was the premier storyteller among storytellers. What we will miss the most at our family gatherings are her stories."

The women in my family prevailed and we were able to offer on behalf of Mary Jane something I wish we had offered her more often when she was alive: our love and perspective on who she was to us. Here is an excerpt of what I offered:

"I want to focus now on my sister's unique gift. Just today, in a conversation with one of her friends, she and I decided that Mary Jane was part Imogene Coco and part Phyllis Diller, with a dash of Joan Rivers. She was, at heart, a true comedienne. The Irish have a name for this gift. When I was in Brazil a few years ago, I met two women from Ireland who told me about their mother. "She gets invited to lots of funerals because she has the gift of the 'crack.'" Puzzled, I asked, 'crack? as in 'crack cocaine?' "No. The crack, the wisecrack.'"

To make fun of, to bring challenges down to their proper size, to ridicule, especially oneself, this was Mary Jane. She applied her unique sense of humor to her own challenges and to ours. Her skill, which we will miss especially at family gatherings, is to tell the story again and again and again. To keep telling those moments of embarrassment, and fear, and sorrow, until what seemed a tragedy at the time becomes funny, hilarious even, and evidence of the triumph of what we have survived. She reminds us that the joker, the clown, the jester were the only ones who could tell the truth to the king. As her older "recovering too-serious sister," I can say she continually inspired me to stop giving energy to the things that don't matter.

So, what is the wisdom in the wise crack? First off, it's the truth that everything has cracks—it's part of the design. The truth, despite what we want to show the world, is that we have cracks. It's part of our design. And as the poet Leonard Cohen's song Anthem teaches us: *Ring the bells that still can ring/ Forget your perfect offering/ There is a crack, a crack in everything/ That's how the light gets in.*

And I will add, as Mary Jane showed us again and again, it's how the light is able to shine out, too.

Artist Resource

Spoken Word Sounds

There are two main purposes of verbal communication: express feelings and ideas and to be understood. Though counterintuitive, using just sounds in a made-up language, while including gestures and facial expressions, can sometimes work better than attempting to find the right words. The art of speaking without words is called "grammelot." It's an imitation of the sounds of spoken language. A made up in the moment gibberish, it copies the rhythm and intonation of a spoken message while adding only gestures and facial expressions to deliver its message. For Italian street performers in the early part of the sixteenth century, grammelot made it possible to bypass the many languages their European audiences spoke to achieve common understanding. This technique also got them past the censors as they attempted to tell the truth to the king.

Journalist Gabriel Rom, in an article in *The New York Times*, described gibberish's main advantage to the speaker: "There is raw, ridiculous power in expressing oneself through noise alone." In InterPlay, we use a version we call "soul language" to express the feelings associated with the story we are telling, or we call on the nonsense syllables when the expression of emotion in the telling feels beyond words. A bonus: this tool makes it possible to maintain privacy on particulars of the matter, protecting both the innocent and the guilty.

Playback Theater

This type of improvisational theatre begins with an overarching theme and a volunteer audience member telling a story that related to the theme from their life to the company's director. Company members then playfully enact the story on the spot, using one of the playback theatre forms. The audience member and the entire audience watch the company playback the story and reflect on any insights that may emerge. The first Playback Theatre was founded in 1975 by Jonathan Rox and Jo Salas who were influenced by the psychodrama method of Jacob Moreno and the work of educator Paulo Freier. As of 2022, there are fifty-five active companies performing around the world. Locate a company near you.

Reflection/Action

1. Think of a situation or person you are struggling with and talk about it to yourself out loud using "soul language." Just sounds, syllables, gestures, no actual words. Allow yourself to notice and take in your body's reaction to doing this (feelings, energy level, any discoveries, or surprises). Part 2: try this out with a willing partner, taking turns sharing with one another your reactions and understandings as witnesses and speakers.

2. Write a letter to a deceased loved one or someone from your past that you have lost touch with. Then light a candle and read it aloud to yourself. The following day, write what you imagine your friend or loved one's response to you would be. Another variation is to write a letter to your younger self, or your future self. No planning ahead, just begin writing and stay open to what comes.

3. Enlist the help of another person who is willing to take turns telling and witnessing three-sentence stories related to an agreed upon grief or loss theme. Try simple words such as *work, children, health, self-care, home, rest*. Begin with exchanging one item, "I could talk about… [name something]" but don't actually talk about it yet. This will help you establish a menu of possibilities. Next, take turns saying more about one of those somethings, providing more details in three or four sentences, while the other person stays present and holds space for the speaker. Finally, exchange what you noticed when speaking and listening.

Chapter Ten

Dance: Embodying Grief and Its Transformation

My youngest brother Kenny disappeared a few days before his twenty-seventh birthday. He had invited our youngest sister, Maureen, to visit him in New Mexico, but when she arrived, he wasn't there. He had moved to the area from Kentucky to support the local Native American tribe as they reinstituted the Sun Dance, a ceremony that had been banned by federal law since 1884. The dance was due to begin in a few days. The rented teepee he was living in still held his belongings, but there were no other signs of him. On a walk the next day, Maureen found the remains of his dog. He had been shot.

Police were notified, and our parents visited the area that fall and did their own research, finding people to talk with who knew him. After that trip, my father took me aside and said quietly, "I don't know what happened to him, but he's not alive." Meanwhile, Mother laid awake nights, constructing possible scenarios where Ken could still be alive though not in touch with us. *A car accident that resulted in amnesia? Was he in a Mexican jail after driving across the border where authorities found pot in his glove compartment?* Mother sent donations to orders of religious nuns and brothers asking for prayers.

The following fall, we were notified that two hunters found a body in the wooded mountains of New Mexico under two seasons of layered leaves. Dental records confirmed the remains belonged to Kenny. Our long nightmare of uncertainty, fear, and worry had come to an end, and our anticipatory grief transformed into the deep sorrow of final loss. We held a funeral and a burial, but not before the immediate family— two parents and five siblings—gathered around the body bag that contained his remains. Our mother's peace-loving son had died violently. Death had come from a bullet fired at close range to the back of his head, indicating an execution-style killing.

Standing in a circle around his remains in a space at the funeral home, we shared stories of our family's "golden child," Kenny, the fifth of six children. In honor of his having done alternative service in a hospital as a conscientious objector during the Vietnam War, and his interest in the Sun Dance, we performed a folk dance together known then as a *Sufi Dance*, now called one of the *Dances of Universal Peace*. In that time of horror and disintegration, moving together in an orderly, rhythmic connection with one another offered a balm of reassurance that living well beyond that moment could and would be possible.

The outcome of dance is relief, release, sometimes relaxation, and, eventually, joy. Looking back I see how we used dance as a way to reclaim our own joy and pride in our brother. How he stood up against what he considered an unjust war in Vietnam, and later offered support to the native community as they reinstated their ceremonial Sun Dance. I see a connection with what Barbara Holmes, an African American faculty member at the Center for Action and Contemplation tells us about Black joy: "This is not 'joy' in the ordinary sense of the word... This is the communal

174

performance of resistance and resilience through dancing and rhythmic movement... it's defiance of death and the society that produces it."

The popular notion of dance is that it is an energetic celebration of positive moments in life, like weddings, birthdays, and graduations, but less well-known is that dance can also be an act of mourning, a full-bodied communal expression of life's challenges and ways to grapple with them. It is a dual strength of dance that it can help us navigate all our milestone events, which are often a mixture of joy and grief, laughter and tears. This is something my husband and I learned a few years later when we called on another Dance of Universal Peace to invite family members to dance at our wedding.

Nobody thought it was a good idea for us to get married. Some relatives had to overcome their grief in order to be there. Rich's Jewish family did not want him to marry a non-Jew, especially a woman who brought three children with her into the marriage. My Irish-Catholic mother felt she needed to get permission from her priest to even attend the wedding since this was my second marriage, and my first husband was still alive. We couldn't find a rabbi to perform the ceremony, and I didn't ever bother to try and find a priest. Even some friends said, "Why would you want to ruin your relationship by getting married?" When we told the unitarian minister who agreed to perform the ceremony of people's objections, he said, "Once you're married, they'll all get over it."

Most everybody did get over it, and I believe the group dance that we did together as a family at the wedding should get some of the credit. The Dances of Universal Peace are simple, meditative, multicultural, circle dances that use chants, music, and phrases from many spiritual traditions around the globe. Rather than having religious differences become instruments of separation and division, the dances honor the many paths people take to the Divine or to Transcendent Reality. By participating in the dance, people embody the deeper shared values in all spiritual traditions and connect to their own compassionate and loving sides. We chose a particular dance and organized it in such a way that required members of my Catholic/Protestant family to hold hands and dance in an outer circle surrounding the inner circle where Rich's Jewish family members held hands and danced together. At points in the dance, the two circles stopped rotating and individuals from each of the two circles faced one another, paired up and danced together. By the end of the dance, our two families had become one.

Also featured was a song that expressed our hopes for our relationship's future and our belief in the power of dance. It was a gift that, starting out, we didn't see the challenges that lay ahead. But we did know for certain that all and most everything would change, so that's why we pledged to dance. "Let it be a dance we do / May I have this dance with you? / Through the good times and the bad times, too / let it be a dance we do."

In Western culture, we often think of our bodies as just the way our heads and logical brains get transported from one place to another, but for those who dance, the body is the vehicle to experience and express the energy that is moving through it. The body is also what is impacted by the loss of a loved one, leaving the bodies of those that remain at risk for illness, disability, and disease. The expression "dying of a broken heart" has some scientific truth behind it since a mourner's immune system is depressed in the months and years following a death or other significant loss.

At the time my brother's body was recovered, I was teaching family therapy to social work students while also, in one of those unexplainable and jaw-dropping coincidences, working with a Native American community in western Nebraska. My family's grief journey had been so long already before we learned of his death that, looking for some reassurance or certainty, I asked a forties-something Native American leader, "How long should grief last?" His answer: "The elders say eight seasons."

"Uh, two years." I liked that his culture had a timeframe, but I also knew that the circumstances of my brother's death — that it occurred because of a crime — might prolong the time needed to process it.

The following year, as I was teaching my social work class on family systems, I used the story of my brother's disappearance and death to discuss the potential effects of the loss of a family member on the remaining members. To illustrate our situation, I made a list on the blackboard of the effects on the physical health of our family members within six months of the recovery of Kenny's body. Beside the name "Mother," I wrote "heart attack." Beside sister "Maureen," I wrote "emergency trip to the ER with a burst ovary." Beside Mary Jane, "surgery on her esophagus." Beside Dad's name, "kidney stones," and beside my name I wrote, "colitis."

Though mostly healthy before and after, we each responded to the loss of our loved one in a physical and unique way. As I viewed the list from the back of the room, I saw something incomprehensible to our individualistic culture¬: we as family members seemed to be reacting as one organism, each carrying the wound from Kenny's tragic death in a different part of our individual bodies.

Alice Walker said it best in the title of her 2010 poetry book: *Hard Times Require Furious Dancing*. When a friend texted me an image of the book's cover, it reminded me of this beautiful work and its author, whom I've had the honor and pleasure of meeting several times in my life. Seeing the dancing figures on the cover caused me to admit to myself that yes, dancing nearly every day gets me through most any tough time.

Dance and the Healthy Body and Brain

When I was sent to my room by the pandemic, with the help of tech savvy colleagues, my dance studio became transformed into my media studio, allowing me to teach InterPlay classes online and connect with my then eight-year-old granddaughter Kyra several times a week. As part of each session and in the times in between, when I'm waiting for the pot on the stove to boil, or for a phone call to be patched through, I'm likely standing, stretching, and moving to music or without music. Sometimes with students and clients, I refrain from calling this "dancing," lest we fall into the cultural judgements of who gets to dance and how skilled one must be to attempt it. We could call it simply "movement," as in "keep moving," something our bodies, minds, and spirits need for health. I often share what the editor of my first book, Frances Townsend, taught me: "Our blood has a pump, the heart, but everything else—your lymph system, your digestive system, your elimination system—moves around when you do."

So, moving our bodies in a rhythmic manner is central to gaining and maintaining health, to keep the stressful energy from settling into our bones and bodies. We dance to calm our emotional upheavals, grieve our losses, and move painful energy out beyond our individual energetic fields, lest by holding onto the effects of past atrocities we keep them alive.

Confirmation from Science

No dance performed by a successful prospector in the moment of discovering gold could rival the happy dance I did in my kitchen when I realized the motherlode of evidence I discovered on the effects of dance on health as I was preparing a presentation on "Move Your Body, Improve Your Mind." Not one, not two, but six reports of studies, some of which were meta-analyses of many studies, demonstrated the positive effects of dance and other mind-body movement regimes on the brain.

- One eight-year study of over 1,000 elderly Japanese women looked at how physical activity affected the women's ability to carry on tasks of daily living. The researchers found **women who danced frequently had a 73% lower chance of becoming disabled.**

- In the *Journal of American Geriatric Society,* I found a meta-analysis of 32 randomized controlled trials with 3,624 participants that looked at the effects of mind-body exercises on cognitive function in older adults. The results? **Dance and Tai Chi improved global recognition, cognitive flexibility, working memory, verbal fluency, and learning in both cognitively intact and impaired older adults.**

- One 2017 study divided older adults into three groups after measuring their brain's matter. One group engaged in dance, the other two in walking and balance training regimes. **Only the dance group that engaged in country dance three times a week for an hour showed an improvement in the white matter of the brain.** (White

179

matter is the group of cells that pass messages on to the neurons.) The white matter tends to fray and deteriorate as we age and is thought to be related to cognitive decline.

• A study reported in the *New England Journal of Medicine* compared various leisure activities and the risk of dementia in the elderly. Subjects were a prospective cohort of 469 subjects older than 75 years and who did not have dementia at the baseline measurement. **Dancing was the only physical activity associated with a lower risk of dementia.**

• 1,071 studies were screened. Dance increased hippocampal volume, gray matter volume, and white matter integrity. Functional changes included alterations in cognitive functioning—improvement in memory, attention, body balance, psychosocial parameters, and altered peripheral neurotrophic factor. In short, **dance integrates brain areas to improve neuroplasticity.**

Living Differently

One of my favorite poems in Alice Walker's book is *Calling All Grandmothers,* and begins:

"We have to live differently, or we will die in the same old ways." To me, living differently means recognizing the potential effects of loss on our physical health, our ongoing need for movement and the expression of feelings, and the value of movement and dance.

Walker states something that many people would say: "I have learned to dance. It isn't that I didn't know how to dance before... I just didn't know how basic it is for maintaining balance," to have a vital and satisfying life.

I learned to dance at three years old—a lifetime gift from my mother, who gave me what her mother would not allow her: dancing lessons. I took my mother's love of dance and made it my own, taking dancing further than she had intended. As a teenager, I left home to study, and as a young adult, traveled the country as a professional dancer. I took dancing further than I even thought possible, and I kept on dancing through periods of struggle and strife, or whenever I didn't know what else to do. No matter what was going on in my life or in the culture of my life with others, I felt better and more able to carry on by dancing.

I've been more than a little curious for years about what has caused so many people in Western culture to adopt the sentiments of the song, "I *won't* dance, don't ask me!" or, "I *can't* dance." (I'm too old, too fat, have no rhythm, or have two left feet!) When I lived in Texas, I visited a university in the so-called "Bible Belt" and was told that the charter for the university did not allow dancing on the campus. Perhaps that's why some have chosen not to dance, though it overlooks the fact that the biblical King David was known "to dance before the Lord." In addition to dancing, the university charter also forbade drinking, cussing, and card playing. Not sure of the order of the list, but I have had clients and students tell me that dancing was forbidden by their religion.

Walker directs all grandmothers to, "Step forward and assume the role for which you were created: to lead humanity to health, happiness, and sanity." For the sake of my own health, happiness, and sanity, I've been dancing in my dance studio, now turned media studio, on the ground floor of my home, most days since the global pandemic hit in March of 2020. I invited others to join me. We have explored our own self-care while taking care of others and as we have been confronted by a tsunami of losses. Through the magic of Zoom, coming

181

together from cities, countries, and continents, we have danced and shaken off the dread and fear that surrounded us.

Movements We Call Dance

Dance involves moving the body in space rhythmically, often accompanied by music, for the purpose of expressing an idea or emotion, to release energy, or just to delight in the movements themselves. A review of folk dances from different countries reveals some categories¬ related to weather. Dancers in cold climates tend to engage in lots of stomping motions to keep warm. People in warmer climates approach dance with gentle wave-like motions, perhaps to lessen the possibility of becoming overheated.

In InterPlay, we play with the Four Movement Patterns of thrust, shape, hang, and swing that make up all movement. Identified initially in the 1920s by physical education researchers at UCLA, these kinesthetic patterns could be described as the "primary colors" that, when put together, make up all movement. According to the work of kinesiologists Judith Rathbone and Valerie Hunt, most anyone and everyone can perform each of the patterns, but due to the unique way each person's body communicates with their brain, and the way neurons fire in their muscles, most people have a strong preferred pattern as well as a less preferred or weaker one.

Dance educator Betsy Wetzig and aikido coach Ginny Whitelaw connected the patterns to psychological and behavioral attitudes that seem to accompany them in their book on leadership, *Move to Greatness: Focusing the Four Essential Energies of a Whole and Balanced Leader.*

Swing movements involve a lift and a drop, often from side to side. Such movements are quite evident in the social dances that developed from the swing style of jazz music in the 1920s-1940s. "It don't mean a thing, if it ain't got that swing." This pattern encourages collaboration, and friends I know who have strong elements of swing are frequently connecting people to one another: "You need to meet..." "Have you heard of...?" Without enough swing, a person may experience isolation and loneliness.

Thrust movements move out directly and forcefully in all directions from the lower abdomen and can include stomping motions into the ground. Flamenco dancers accompanying themselves with castanets, and Maori dancers of New Zealand, waving knives and swords, move with percussive yet graceful intensity and speed. People with a strong element of thrust get to the point in a conversation and frequently meet their goals. Without enough thrust, a person may experience a lack of urgency or focus.

Hang movements are prominent in hip hop dancing. The physical body center for this movement pattern is diffuse and free-floating. Ecstatic trance dancers emphasize hang as they follow their kinesthetic senses. We say we are "hanging out" when we're leaning back together without a focused assignment or purpose. In Wetzig and Whitelaw's description, the hanger is a visionary with a soft focus and 180-degree vision, open to new things. Without enough hang, a person can lack flexibility and openness. With too much, it's difficult to get things done.

Shape movements are prominent in ballet, yoga, and classical Indian dance where a relaxed stillness is achieved in various postures with graceful movements between them. Shapers are organizers, able to see next steps, but at risk for perfectionism if the need for shape becomes too much. Without enough shape, we risk becoming disorganized. Too much shape and we drive other people crazy with our fussbudgety focus on details.

Dance as a Sacred Art

Images of dancing figures are present even in the oldest of cave paintings (in India, dating to 8000 BCE, and in Egyptian tomb paintings dating to 3300 BDC), so it's likely that dance evolved together with the other arts. For early people, dance was religious in nature as it connected them to one another and to their gods, to the forces of nature, or to whatever they considered life's larger realities.

Like the visual and musical arts, dance expresses what we don't have words for. It communicates through a universal language of the soul. The intention to connect with what Native Americans call the "Great All That Is," "All Our Relations" is what transforms the dancers and those that witness them into conduits of faith, peace, and love. So, dance would seem a natural art to enhance people's religious experiences.

Most religious organizations in Western culture no longer forbid dance outright, though most have trouble welcoming it into their worship services. As a student in Catholic schools, I was invited to sing in the church choir at masses for weddings and funerals, but though dance was a class in my high school where attendance earned students physical education credits, there were no movement choirs in the churches. Despite that, I had a strong connection to dance as a sacred art through my dance teacher in Louisville who had been a student of Ruth St. Denis and Ted Shawn in their Denishawn School. That school, founded in 1914, ushered in a new era of modern dance, drawing from Asian and indigenous cultures to connect the physical with the spiritual. When I was sixteen, my teacher secured an entire summer's scholarship at the Jacob Pillow Dance Festival for my best friend Mimi and I, where we met in person then elders Shawn (64) and St. Denis (76).

Ushering in the theatre watching Ruth St. Denis transform every night from a bent over little old lady into a breathtakingly beautiful goddess figure transformed me and my view of dance and what age you must be to do it. As she stood, often in profound stillness, projecting an ageless beauty, it was impossible to take your eyes off her. When I think of the term "embodied presence," that state of being in one's body so completely that it becomes the gateway to your creativity and aliveness, I remember those performances of the dancer Ruth St. Denis and how she was the personification of it.

Dance Performed on Behalf of the Mourners

In addition to dancing to process our own feelings and emotions, we can dance on behalf of others, helping them to process their feelings and emotions. When a dancer physically expresses feelings and ideas, they are communicated to the viewer directly, bypassing words. This is due to a distinctive class of neurons that fire both when we execute a movement and when we *observe* someone else performing the same or similar act. These *mirror neurons* create an exchange of body language which needs no words.

Knowing this, we members of the InterPlay community call on one another for support in processing life experiences such as loss and grief. I might ask someone to dance on my behalf regarding an issue or difficulty I am going through. When someone tells me of a challenge they are experiencing, I might offer to dance on their behalf. When we can observe one another's dances, we often make amazing discoveries— things we wouldn't have thought of in our logical minds. These empathic exchanges are ways we companion one another and share our bodies' wisdom—an example of "the part of us that is smarter than we are."

Dancing to Explore Difficult Themes

My fellow InterPlay improv artists and I often play with challenging individual and cultural topics — grief and sorrow, love and loss — and we have performed as a part of juried art shows, dancing and storytelling in art galleries and at conference where the topics of violence against women and the sigma of mental illness are being explored and represented. Our individual and collective expression comes from our bodies' wisdom, knitted together in forms of creative connection. Whether we're online or in person, after we've created and performed a sequence together, someone will say, "That was so satisfying," and we all agree that it was.

It was June 1967. As a founding member of the Festival Dancers out of the Jewish Community Center in Detroit, I gathered with members of the company in the sanctuary of an Episcopal church in the suburbs. We were preparing to dance to Leonard Bernstein's *Chichester Psalms.* In those days, before instant messaging and cell phones, someone told us the news that Israel had just been attacked and was at war with Jordan, Syria, and Egypt. One of our company members, Shirley, was absent from us as she was traveling in Israel at the time.

The company members created a circle formation facing inward on the platform, and with arms encircling one another's waist, we bowed our heads to pray. I can still see the long narrow center aisle of the church as parishioners began slowly streaming into the pews. As I write this, I can revisit the feelings of fear, the unevenness of my breath, the worry that hung palatable in the air around us. We said out loud to one another that we would dance on behalf of Shirley, her family, and all those involved. The dance was our prayer for their safety, and that the hostilities would end quickly.

Costumed in long dresses that recapitulate the colors in the stained-glass windows, we took our opening positions. Arms raised upward towards the ceiling forming a V, heads turned to the side as in an ancient Egyptian relief carving, we entered the sanctuary from stage left. As we took three steps in unison into the sanctuary, the choir began singing in Hebrew the psalm, "Make a joyful noise unto the Lord."

After the eighteen-minute dance, I was still in a trance as we gathered again in a circle in a small side room hung with choir robes. I realized that I had not danced as I had done many times before—the steps, the choreography, my body knew them all well. As the choreographer's assistant, much of the piece had been worked out on my body, and company members, and the director and choreographer Harriet Berg all relied on my body to remember its routine. I taught the steps to new dancers and revised the piece to accommodate the various settings we performed it in. But on that day, I had not danced. From the first note of the music to the last, I was in total surrender to what my body and my spirit knew so well. Instead of being the dancer, I became the dance. The dance danced me.

Throughout my life since, I have sought out opportunities to learn to do something so well, and for a deep enough purpose, that I could let go into allowing myself to be danced to its conclusion. Looking at this through the eyes of a grief advocate, this seems a worthwhile life goal—to allow the dance of life to dance me. With gratitude, not resistance, to what comes. To do what my friend Lu Curtis saw me do once, while dancing at our women's retreat. As I was dancing, the photograph of my son Kenneth who was living with AIDS at the time, caught the corner of my eye, and I picked it up and continued the dance while clutching it to my chest. "You've just demonstrated my religion!" Lu Curtis said. "I'm a Sufi and we're taught, whatever life hands you, pick it up and dance with it."

The dance doesn't have to be beautiful, just an authentic expression of our souls, that which makes us uniquely who we are—the essential you of you and the essential me of me. I encourage you to let go of any thoughts or self-consciousness about your skills or what your movements will look like. Dance as though no one is watching and try the following movement activity in the Reflection/Action section below.

Artist Resource

My brother Miles, knowing of my dedication to the role that the arts can play in helping us grieve, sent me the link to an amazing example of what witnessing someone dancing grief can be like. The three-minute film, crafted from over thirty hours of footage, is a *New Yorker* documentary titled *Unspoken*. One of dance's biggest advantages is that it does not rely on words but comes from a deeper place of clear awareness. As each of the arts do, dance connects to universal themes and large-scale human dilemmas. In the art of dance, the dancer Sebastian Haynes, with assistance from the music of composer Alexander McKenzie, embodies the emotion and energy of grief itself. This embodied expression communicates to the viewer, and through the magic of mirror neurons, the performer carries the viewer or witnesses into the dance with him.

The film begins with the international choreographer, Paul Lightfoot, speaking about how he is hoping that the dance he is making could be a way for him to say goodbye to his father. He was unable to do that when his father died in a hospital during Covid when visitors were not allowed.

Filmmaker William Armstrong, who was looking for a story to tell that reflected the uncertainty and fear of that cultural moment, came together with Lightfoot, musician Alexander McKensie, and an especially athletic and exquisitely skilled male dancer. Viewing the dance that was constructed and performed on Zoom takes us, the witnesses, on a full-bodied expressive journey of loss and longing, sorrow, and invigorating resistance, ending in quiet acceptance of what is lost and what is found.

Resource for Dance as Therapy

Movement is both an assessment tool and a primary mode of intervention for dance therapists, according to the American Dance Therapy Association. The field was established in the 1940s, when professional dancers like Mariam Chase began exploring using dance and movement as a form of psychotherapy, offering dance to patients in mental health facilities.

Reflection/Action

Movements to Dance Your Grief

In online classes during the pandemic, my students and I explored ways to use movement and dance to process loss. Sometimes we would begin with a specific loss and then see what movements our bodies spontaneously came up with. This works well and especially when witnessed and reflected upon, can have a profound outcome for both witness and mover. Since the body-mind connection functions in a reciprocal way, we also perform specific types of movement to represent a principle or truth about the grieving process itself. Here are the directions for that exploration. Again, witnessing and reflecting afterwards increases effect.

1. It's said that grief is love with nowhere to go. Explore **reaching** and stretch your arms out in various directions as an expression of **longing**.

2. The mourner is now the one in need of love. Explore movements of **self-soothing** and **hugging** yourself: Wrap your arms around yourself. Take that hug in as you are both the giver and the receiver. Recognize that you are loved.

3. Mourners need to fully recognize the reality of their loss. As a master of a self-defense system acknowledges a worthy opponent, explore creating the movements of a formal **bow**. We practice **bowing** to what is totally beyond our control.

4. A significant loss unleashes strong energies in ourselves and in the people and systems of which we are a part. Explore becoming an instigator of strong energy by lifting your arms and dropping them in movements of **swing**. Notice how the more forcefully you drop your arms, the easier the lift. After exploring the movements of a large swing, hold onto your shoulders and use a **gentle swinging motion** to rock yourself.

5. The loss was not what you wanted, not what you expected or preferred. **Thrust** your arms outward with strong energy into the space around you, while exhaling and allowing sounds to accompany the movement. Stomp your feet into the floor, as in marching or tap dancing. Switch to flamenco style dancing to evoke passionate feelings of sadness and love.

6. We do not have to grieve alone. Practice allowing yourself to be held by exploring the movements of **hang**. Lean on your desk, then on a chair, then against a nearby wall. Allow the top of your body to go limp, relying on gravity to hold you up. Think about who and what you can rely on now.

7. Rather than holding still, give yourself the gift of stillness by exploring **shape and stillness:** Create a shape with your arms or your whole body and imagine you are giving yourself the gift of stillness in that shape. Create another shape and allow a soft stillness to overtake you. After a few breaths, ask yourself the question: "To what life is this loss calling me?"

8. Wait in the stillness for an answer.

Chapter Eleven

Music and Voice: Resonating and Resolving Grief

My grandsons, Ethan and Will, were nine and six years old respectively when I watched their mother interrupt a fight they were having. She had clearly done this before, and I saw that she had some skill in getting the boys to each look at the situation from the other's point of view. After some discussion, she instructed them to each apologize to one another. Ethan, the eldest, went first. With his head cocked to the side, he said, "I'm sorry."

Will came back quickly and strong with, "Oh no, you're not! You're just over there singing to yourself."

I was able to stay in my role as fair witness, but it was hard not to laugh and somewhat agree with Will because I knew that, as a musically inclined child, Ethan did sing to himself often. I've always wondered if that's how he keeps himself in such an even-tempered and emotionally positive place.

Those boys are grown men now. There are many principles I hope I have shared with them, many truths I would like them to remember and embody, with one of the most important being that *the capacity of music to facilitate a change in one's emotional state is enormous.* As we know from

African American spirituals, known as "sorrow songs," and from a more recent form of music, the blues, music can express for us the emotions inherent in our grief, and take us in a progression from negative to positive, from discordant to resolved.

Physician Oliver Sachs, author of *Musicophia: Tales of Music and the Brain,* reminds us that "music occupies more areas of the brain than language does — humans are a musical species." It can be hard to find the right words to describe the progress on our grief journeys. Hopefully, most people know that the goal is not to "get over it" and "move on." Sometimes we talk about "healing" our grief, but grief isn't an illness, so unless we are referring to the trauma associated with some losses that needs healing that word doesn't fit. Arriving at a "resolution" has possibilities, except that word usually means finding a solution to a problem or a puzzle. And grief, though it can be puzzling, is not a problem to be solved.

As I learned more about music, I got excited by the possibility that music theory might have a suggestion for us. In Western tonal music theory, the term "resolution" is the move of a note or chord from dissonance (an unstable sound) to a consonance (a more final or stable sounding one). That fits with grief — a journey from and through instability to stability. That got me thinking about what music offers our grief journeys, not just as a metaphor but as medicine. Could music bring us through an episode of grief to a resolution, for now? As with other arts, can music be a vehicle to take us into our grief, help us process it, and bring us out?

As happens often when I set out wholeheartedly on a path of discovery, the universe starts providing me resources. I came across two women who each had had music as a support system for their lives since childhood, and now find it useful in their lives as elders. Rebecca is a pianist whose mother and grandmother played classical music and who introduced her to music early in her life. She described music as her medicine. "When I was a kid, I felt music understood me in a way that people couldn't –music understood longings and sorrows I couldn't possibly tell anyone or even put into words. We talked about the message of reassurance in the chord resolution, which is when traditional chord resolution brings us home and we are changed." We talked about the message of reassurance in the chord resolution, which is when the chord resolution brings us home.

I asked Rebecca about something I'd found in my search to connect music with grief, something known as the tension and release in music. "This refers to the build-up of musical intensity that eventually dissolves and relaxes," she explained. "A moment of unrest in the music creates an expectation for its resolution and an anticipation for the drama to resolve. Tension and release keep the music moving forward."

For me, this tension and release connects with one of the newer theories on grief: The Dual Process Model of Grief. This model, originating in the mid-nineties by Margaret Stroebe and Henk Schut, sees the work of grieving as two-sided: 1) The loss orientation where a person processes the loss through remembering, yearning, and reminiscing to let go of the relationship bonds, and 2) The restoration-orientation, which includes coping with secondary losses, and rebuilding a life after the loss. The main feature of this model is the notion that it's healthy to oscillate between the two, experiencing grief in doses. This is where self-care comes in. It's care for oneself and what's needed at the time that regulates the oscillation. Just as the tension and releasing keeps the music moving forward, oscillation keeps the grief moving.

For my friend Cathy, being in a choir or chorus has been a central part of her social-emotional life since middle school. But now, as an elder, taking care of her ninety-two-year-old mother, and with the restrictions of Covid, she hasn't found a replacement in her present life for what singing has always done. "I sing in the car, but it's not the same."

Cathy mentioned she had been experimenting with the vocal form of toning, a kind of sound healing to "recalibrate" her energy level. That word caught my attention, and I looked it up as we were online together and read its definition out loud. "To adjust the gradations or settings on a piece of precious equipment." We both laughed and agreed that our bodies, minds, and spirits could be considered pieces of precious equipment. And music just might be a way to recalibrate our losses from the past and our expectations for the future.

My friend Mitch, a musician and composer who earned his living as a mathematician and mathematics professor, shared that he noticed music can sometimes make us laugh. "If you've ever been part of a jazz group or witnessed one close-up, you've probably seen times when one player performs a solo and the other members of the group let out a chuckle, along with murmurs of approval."

He asks, "What's that about? There were no words. Nobody did a pratfall. Somehow, the music itself told a joke. The notes leading up to the joke were a set-up, getting our heart in the right place to be tickled." And then he points us to classical music. "It works the same way. Check Rachmaninov's Rhapsody on a theme by Paganini. It tickles."

So, as we wish for something better in times of grief and loss, we can look to music and singing to provide a way to honor our struggles and make our lives feel better, even if nothing has changed in our objective reality.

Some of my questions about how music provides us with catharsis, solace, connection, and sometimes feel-good joy were answered when I met Gary Malkin, the Emmy award-winning composer and musician. "We're vibratory beings," Gary said. To demonstrate, he showed a thirty-second video of chaotic city life with a music soundtrack that matched the rhythm and tone of the clattering trains, taxicab traffic, and helter-skelter patterns of pedestrians dodging one another on the sidewalks of New York City. Next, he replayed the same video, but changed our experience of it entirely by replacing the soundtrack with an orchestral version of Pachelbel's Canon. Our eyes still brought us chaos, but the soothing music kept our bodies calm and collected.

If we are vibratory beings, what do the vibrations of music itself do for us? Through a friend of a friend, I met Monique Mead, a violin professor at Carnegie Mellon and an accomplished musician with a passion for using music to induce the positive feelings of relaxation. During the pandemic, Monique and other musicians held outdoor porch concerts in their neighborhood during the summers when everyone was house bound. Once it became possible to gather indoors, Monique established and outfitted a place to hold sound healing sessions. I couldn't wait to try out this simple edgy method of what might be labeled self-healing.

Sound does not come to us just through our ears. As friends and I experienced last weekend at a group session, sound is physically felt through vibrations in the body. As the human body is seventy-five percent water, our bodies are great conductors of the vibrations created by musical instruments. Monique plays, in addition to her violin, Tibetan and crystal bowls, a gong, bells, and an ocean drum, and maybe some others I didn't identify. Our bodies vibrate at the same frequency as the sounds produced by the musical instruments, so as Monique plays, physical and emotional tensions held in the body release. Scientists would say that the sound frequencies slow down brainwaves to a restorative state, which activates the body's self-healing system.

During my first sound bath session, my awareness of an area of my upper jaw where I knew I had chronically held tension in years past was heightened. The sensation was not at the level of pain, but definitely uncomfortable. As the session progressed, the sensation diminished, and by the end, it was completely gone. At my second session, the sensation of tension returned in the same place, but it was much less prominent, and it dissipated more quickly. During my third session Friday evening, where I brought several friends with me, the sensation and tension did not occur at all. But something else quite remarkable did. By the middle of the third session, in the place where those tense sensations had been, I began feeling a sensation of openness, like the cells had room to breathe. I thought, Is this how my upper jaw is supposed to be? *Is this the normal vibratory frequency of these cells when I'm not unconsciously clamping down on them?*

Text messages from the friends that accompanied me to the session streamed in the following morning. "Slept great!!" (From someone who can't make that statement often.) Another: "Two months ago: diagnosis bursitis, right shoulder. Last night and today: 90% improvement in pain reduction and range of motion. Sound healing! Hallelujah!" A third¬: "Thank you for organizing us!"

In the interest of full disclosure, my friends and I spent time together after the session, and our individual outcomes may have been influenced by a phenomenon known to bio-musicologists as entrainment, or the synchronization of organisms to an external rhythm. To psychologists, entrainment is defined as the adjustment or moderation of one's behavior to synchronize or be in rhythm with another's behavior. Grief rituals in many cultures provide support partly by taking advantage of this natural rhythmic co-regulation or contagion that happens when bodies come together. "*Group* sound healings! Hallelujah!"

According to Malkin, "Music is the universal language of human emotion and a tool to bring us into presence." I know from my work in improvisation that being fully present is necessary for all that we know to be fully available to us in each present moment. Gary thinks too many people have trouble being fully present because they suffer from "Awareness Fragmental Disorder," an element of what he calls the "psycho-emotional-spiritual epidemic of our times." He sees people in our culture experiencing dangerous imbalances between doing and being (work and life), over-engaging with digital devices, involved in hyper-linear rational processing and youth-obsessed avoidance of facing illness, death and dying, grief and trauma. He sees his music as addressing this epidemic.

I was familiar with Gary's earlier work *Graceful Passages*, with musicians Michael and Doris Stillwater and its musical soundtrack that provides ease to those involved in the dying process. Newer musical programs include *Care for the Journey*, alleviating stress for healthcare providers, and *Safe in the Arms of Love*, which enhances parents' bonds with newborns.

When looking for tools to process human emotion, we find that music may be the most ubiquitous and pervasive tool of all. A 2022 study conducted by the International Federation of the Phonographic Industry concluded that music fans spend an average of 20.1 hours weekly listening to music on multiple formats, including radio, video, television, film, and gaming. A 2017 study found people listen to music while doing other things. Younger generations listen to music outdoors while walking or running or working out at the gym. Many people bring music along as they work or travel on public transportation. For all generations, the most common places to hear music are in homes and automobiles. Since most retail establishments and restaurants have pre-selected playlists entertaining their customers non-stop, it may be more difficult to avoid hearing music when you are longing for a time and place of quiet.

From the point of view of grieving, music can be a potent carrier and igniter of strong emotions and memories. It's quite common for someone whose relationship with their significant other has just ended to be caught unawares and overcome by the emotions of grief when unannounced, they hear what they considered their "special song." Or when a recently deceased loved one's favorite artist is featured unexpectedly on the video or film you happen to be watching.

It helps if you know that this sudden feeling of "coming unglued" that can happen most any place—as you are driving in your car or walking in the mall—has a name and a perfectly logical explanation. Such an experience is known as a "grief burst," and it's good to know that this aspect of music's superpower can serve us well when we purposefully use music as a tool for grieving. When your intention is to access the feelings of grief, to revisit memories that seem to be becoming fainter, or to enhance your gratitude for what you once had in your life, music can serve as your most accessible portal.

If you add up all the music and songs we've heard in our lives, even for a young person, we already have a significant playlist of musical options to call on when we need them. Though I can't say I fully understand how this process works, I have experienced it. One of the most dramatic examples of the way music can reprieve at just the right time occurred when I was at a Gestalt therapy retreat in the Colorado high desert with therapist and author Barry Stevens. Before attending the retreat, I had read her book, *Don't Push the River, It Flows by Itself,* and I knew that this title contained an attitude and skill I needed to acquire. I had mistakenly thought that she was deceased, but when I learned that not only was she alive but that she was offering a retreat that summer, I drove myself from Nebraska to Colorado to work with her.

At the time, I was the mother of three school-aged children and in a place of strong angst about my future. So, when I was offered the chance to work individually with Barry during a group session, I volunteered to bring my life issues forward. As I explained how I was wrestling with the decision of whether to end my twelve-year marriage, and my fear that whatever I decided might hurt my children, Barry guided me into a place of deep listening.

Seated on the dusty ground in view of the red rocks and canyons of Shura, the retreat center, I heard through the hot dry air the silence of the desert. I heard the chirp of a bird, the sound of my own breathing. Then, from inside me, I heard music and lyrics that I recognized as being from a popular Beatles song: "Mother Mary said to me, there will be an answer, let it be, let it be. There will be an answer, let it be." I knew this to be a wise suggestion. Continuing to try and force a decision before I was ready was not going to work. And I marveled at the fact that this came from me, from what I now call "the part of me that is smarter than I am."

"Listening to music takes us to some wonderful places," according to my friend Rebecca. She gives the example of the oboes in the second movement of Bach's first Brandenburg Concerto. "They meet me immediately with grief and hurt, surround me, sing it for me, carry me. And if I couldn't take the dancing cheer of the third movement, I could go back to those wailing oboes."

Then she said something that applies to both music and grief. "It stretches us so much that we are able to take in what follows in the third movement, the joy that floods in."

It's clear that music can cheer us up, help us slow down, remind us of who we are, or who we were in an earlier time, and help us metabolize loss. Some people, like my grandson Ethan, seem to have discovered some of this earlier in their lives than the rest of us.

The Art of Singing

We are on a road trip in the family car, which had to be either a basic no-frills Ford, Chevy, or Plymouth since Dad's company alternated between those three American-made brands when purchasing their company cars every three years. The trip is long enough that one or another of us four kids have repeatedly asked the question, "Are we there yet?"

To pass the time, we begin singing songs from camp or scouts or church choir. It becomes a contest as to who can remember the most words to the songs. At some point, my mother turns her head around from the front seat and casually says over her shoulder, "If you're singing for us, you can stop now." This was often followed by a smirk or a laugh.

This scene was repeated many times on our road trips and in our household—mother's snarky putdowns regarding our singing voices. It wasn't until many years later, when I was making my living in the theater and sometimes having difficulty projecting my voice when called on to sing, that I realized that these discouraging comments were costing me my ability to claim and confidently rely on my own voice. It took some assistance from teachers and much effort on my part to overcome this. I'm certain that these comments and putdowns are what mother's parents or caregivers had said to her, and perhaps what had been said to them. I see this now as part of how many people in Western culture have lost their confidence in the art-based birthright practices of singing, dancing, storytelling, and art-making that can be so helpful for us in processing the experiences of our lives.

I'm happy to report that I didn't pass on that multi-generational putdown to my own children. I was able to fully appreciate and enjoy my daughter Corinne's beautiful voice as she sang as a soloist in her high school chorus, at friends' wedding ceremonies, and even at her own wedding. I got to be the proud mother in the front row when my son Kenneth sang his lead roles in musical comedy theater. And I was present, too, as Ken used music and songs to deliver messages of hope to himself and to me. As he lived and struggled with AIDS, he continually played the song *Seasons of Love* from the musical Rent asking himself the questions the song raises, *"How do you measure a year?*

"How do you measure a year in a life?

It's time now to sing out,

although it's not the end,

to celebrate, remember a year in the life of a friend."

When Ken saw that I was struggling in my role as his companion, or with some other challenge in my work life, he'd slip a cassette containing a song he'd re-recorded into the player in my car. Tears would stream down my face as I listened in the privacy of my own automobile sound studio to "No one's gonna harm you, not while I'm around," a song he had sung to an older woman character in *Sweeney Todd*, or *No One is Alone*, a song sung by a character whose wife has died from the musical *Into the Woods*.

Vocal Play

Voice is a key pathway to discovering our body's wisdom and expressing what is uniquely ours. In InterPlay, we encourage people to make friends with their own voice. We call it "vocal play." No matter what may have happened in one's life to discourage accessing the voice—and incidents like the one I described above are quite common—reclaiming one's voice turns out to be an empowering, often delight-filled activity. The outcome for our sense of wellbeing goes way beyond the immediate situation of playing with our voices in community. Singing and vocal play are excellent vehicles for processing and letting go of the pain and emotional reactions stimulated by grief and loss.

Letting Go of The Past

One of the most challenging grief and loss experiences is to have to downsize from a place that has been home for decades into a smaller, less private place, especially for elders who have accumulated a lifetime of treasured objects. Several years ago, my sister Pat's memory problems made it necessary for her to move from her four-bedroom house into a two-room apartment in an assisted living facility. She and her son needed my help to accomplish that, so I rounded up our siblings to travel to Michigan and spend the Christmas holiday assisting them with this project.

The move was something Pat did not want to do. Some of the time, she subscribed to the wisdom principle that I consider the definition of being a grown up: *What I want changes when I see what the situation requires.* But, as my siblings and I gathered from nearby states to help Pat with the mammoth task before her, she often reverted to the state of mind she was in when she selected each "treasure" for her home. Standing in the center of the room, Pat slowly turned a piece of pottery over in her hands, falling in love with the item all over again. She grabbed a plate from my sister Mary Jane's hands, interrupting her attempt to place white packing paper around it for safe transport to the women's shelter. We tried reminding Pat that we weren't throwing things away. We were selecting things to give away that will help other women in need. We knew she wanted nothing in the landfill.

About the third day of the Christmas holiday, my sisters and I became desperate. Exhausted and on our last nerve, I suddenly remembered my then three-year-old granddaughter Kyra's favorite song from the musical *Frozen*. As we were assembled in the kitchen, sorting items into piles of *Take With*, *Give Away*, and Throw Away, Pat continued to try and stop us from taking her treasures from her. I pulled up the song *Let it Go* on my cell phone and we began singing in rhythm to the activity.

> *Let it go, let it go!*
> *Can't hold it back anymore.*
> (We would then put an object in a pile.)
> *Let it go, let it go!*
> *Turn away and slam the door.*
> (Another item goes in a pile.)
> *I don't care what they're going to say,*
> *let the storm rage on.*
> (Another item goes in a pile.)
> *The cold never bothered me anyway."*

Not sure how many repetitions of this song we went through before our hysterical laughter had us collapsed together in our own people pile on the kitchen floor, but the song and the playful attitude it engendered got us through.

As it turned out, this was the last time we were able to all be together. When we gathered for Pat's memorial, five or so years later, this experience with the song was one of the most enjoyable memories recounted from that most stressful time.

Upon Hearing Bad News

When we are hurting, we need to process the anger and hurt without hurting ourselves or others. Singing, like the other expressive arts, can be a vehicle for doing that, but we need a safe space, and I found such a space in shower stalls. I described an example of this in my previous book, *Warrior Mother:*

> *After hearing of my daughter Corinne's stage three breast cancer diagnosis (after she had been complaining to doctors for five years that something was wrong with her right breast), showers became my venting chambers. No matter where I was staying, the tiny stalls, usually enclosed by glass doors and surrounding tile, provided sound proofing for my howling rage. "WHAT GOOD CAN COME FROM THIS?" I sang to the universe... Like the flexible shower head that can double the force of the water spray or intermittently pulse it, I waited for the song phrase to move around, as song phrases often did, to bring me to a softer place. But "WHAT GOOD CAN COME FROM THIS?" wasn't budging.*

> *As I vocalized daily, the phrase did eventually budge, changing into a plea that became a prayer, "GOOD COULD COME FROM THIS," then a vow, "GOOD WILL COME FROM THIS."*

206

And it did, though the full realization of that goodness has taken decades to realize and will continue to unfold for me throughout my lifetime. I have come to appreciate that the time I had with my daughter, when we were both fully aware of the fact of life's impermanence, of the likelihood of her shortened lifespan, was a time outside of time—what is sometimes called The Eternal Now. This caused us to not go too far ahead, or linger in past regrets, but to live fully, and experience things more deeply than we would have otherwise.

When I think of what singing does for the singer, I'm reminded of a definition for singing that has stayed with me for years. It's a line from a forgotten folk song, "Singing is weeping in the soul." I experienced this function of singing when I was with my daughter in the hospital in Houston. Her treatment journey was not going well, and we had gotten a new round of bad news, so I needed a quiet place where I could experience my frustration and sadness while sheltering her from it. I found the hospital chapel and entered it, hoping it could be that place of quiet where I could compose myself.

I quickly had to let go of my expectations. The small room was filled with African American women arranging themselves into a Christian praise choir for a service that was about to begin. I said to myself, "This can work out. Corinne loves Jesus, and I love to sing, so I can do this." But it turned out that I couldn't.

I discovered its near impossible to sing and cry at the same time. So, I alternated. And it was a good combination. When I was singing, it required my full breath. When I was weeping, my breath was inhibited. But both activities were an expression and a release of my sorrow.

Singing On Our Behalf

After acknowledging the power of using our own voices, we must also recognize that sometimes the art of singing, like all the other performance arts, can be done on our behalf. The singing form of a lament is an expression of and an outpouring of grief. Dating back four thousand years, laments are traditionally sung all over the world by women at funerals and in moments of transition, such as bidding farewell to a loved one. The tone of a lament is a demonstrative expression of sorrow, including disappointment or protest, finding outlet through cries and sounds of loud moaning. Keening is a Gaelic Celtic version of lament performed at the wake and gravesite by professional women singers. Their raucous unearthed emotions and loud moans and cries expressed for the community what they were feeling inside.

At a present-day funeral, those present are put in touch with their own sorrow when the choir or soloist sings the *Ave Maria* or *Amazing Grace,* or in a Jewish context the *Mourner's Kaddish.* As the song's soothing soundwaves wash over those in attendance, they create a communal chamber and people are freed to quietly experience and express their own personal sorrow, which might involve tears, memories, or silent, wordless stillness.

Sacred Containers for Story and Song

My InterPlay improv troupe has played online with a respectful performative way to recount grief experiences. By alternating short snippets of spoken word story with sung lines from a familiar folk song, a sacred container is created. The singing chorus encourages the stories to be connected and gently held. The following written version of the form uses a familiar folk song from the African American tradition. The bold lines are sung.

Michael rowed the boat ashore, hallelujah. Michael rowed the boat ashore, hallelujah.

Our living room had turned into the dying room. Friends linger after stopping by to bring food or flowers. One tells me, "There is so much love in this house. It's hard to leave."

Jordan's river is chilly and cold, hallelujah. Chills the body, but not the soul, hallelujah.

My friend Rose's hospital room in Omaha is now a hospice room. Friends from different cities who'd never previously met meet in that room each evening. We sing songs remembered from girl scout camp or church choir. Since it takes two or three of us to come up with the words to any one song, we laugh a lot, and Rose makes fun of us.

Jordan's river is deep and wide, hallelujah. Got a home on the other side, hallelujah.

A week or so later, when no one is around, I take Rose's hand and begin singing to her a song from my women's spirituality group. "You are woman, you **grow out** of the earth, beautiful, powerful and wise." On the second verse, the words change automatically for me, "You are woman, you go **back** to the earth, beautiful, powerful and wise." At that moment, after fourteen days of her trying to die, Rose let's go.

Jordan's river is deep and wide, hallelujah. Meet my mother on the other side, hallelujah.

Years later, I learn that since the first Threshold Choir began in 1990 in California, there are small groups of people who sing at the bedside of dying persons and that this practice has become a worldwide movement. The singers generate harmonious soundwaves that fill the space, creating a sacred container of love and respect. Their songs make kindness audible, creating a bridge to what lies beyond. Threshold Choir founder Kate Munger described it as "walking each other home."

Michael rowed the boat ashore, hallelujah. Michael rowed the boat ashore, hallelujah.

The pandemic silenced this music at bedsides as it silenced group singing of all types and prohibited familiar in-person bedside rituals of saying goodbye. Hopefully, the re-emergence from isolation after the pandemic has reignited all forms of communal music, especially what the African American leader W.E.B. DuBois called "sorrow songs." As a society, we are emerging souls longing for the balm and encouragement of the many traditions of folk singing and group song.

As we conclude this exploration of music and song as tools for our grieving, let's remember that the capacity of music to facilitate a change in our emotional state is enormous. Recognizing ourselves as "vibratory beings" whose brains are wired to be attuned to rhythmic sounds, we have a clearer understanding of how it works, but the practice of using music and voice to facilitate life transitions for individuals and communities has ancient roots. Music and song have accompanied people into battle and provided the soundtrack for communities to bury their dead. Now, we can intentionally reclaim the superpower that music and voice have to ignite strong emotions, connect us to our memories, and accompany us through the long arc of grieving our losses. As we use the songs we sing to ourselves, and the music that emerges from our own inner playlists, as we share our grief stories and alternate them with sung lines from our favorite folk songs, these art-based practices are helping us live our best lives.

Artist Resource: Mozart's Requiem

The eighteenth-century musician Wolfgang Amadeus Mozart's life gave him much to grieve. Only two of his six children survived. His wife suffered a series of medical crises, leaving him in considerable debt from her expensive spa visits that were the healthcare of that day. A wealthy fellow freemason, Count Waalsegg-Stuppach, commissioned him to compose a requiem as a token of remembrance for the Count's twenty-year-old wife who had died the previous February. Mozart accepted the commission because of his debt, despite being overwhelmed with other assignments and feeling ill while composing the piece. As his health declined, he began to suspect that he was writing the requiem for his own funeral. He continued composing on his deathbed, and when he died, which was a few months short of his thirty-sixth birthday, he left the work unfinished. According to Einstein, who was one of his biggest admirers, "Mozart's music is so pure and beautiful that I see it as a reflection of the inner beauty of the universe."

Resources for Music as Therapy

There is an allied profession known as Music Therapy, made up of credentialed professionals who have completed an approved music therapy program. Practitioners work within a therapeutic relationship to use music interventions to help patients accomplish individualized goals, often in healthcare settings.

Reflection/Action

1. **Lament**: You can begin by writing out the themes of your lament and then taking them to the steps of vocal play, or you can begin by making sounds that eventually lead to song. Start whichever way feels easiest to you.

A) Write First Version - Part One

a) In writing, *name* your loss. Write out your *complaint* to the universe or God or Goddess or whomever seems to be responsible. Next, write your *request* for relief or the desire of your heart now. Use these ideas as you move to vocal play with what you have written.

B) Vocal Play

a) Begin with humming or a tone, allow it to evolve into a one-breath song or a repetitive vocal phrase. Allow it to move as it wants to express the feelings you are experiencing about your loss, then add words to name the loss. Don't worry if it doesn't sound "pretty." Remember, laments were often a noisy form of wailing.

b) You can start your complaining with a rhythm, strike the table or a drum to accompany what you are singing, sounding, or chanting to the universe or God or whomever seems to be responsible.

c) Part Two -Take a breath, and on the exhale, formulate and express in a chant, or with a melody the desire of your heart now.

d) Part Three - Go into stillness with trust and wait.

2. Identify what you are needing in this time in your grief journey and experiment with music that can help provide it. The requiem above could be a choice. Your menu might include music or songs that, for you, match what you are feeling that will then provide solace, catharsis, inspiration, connection, or encouragement.

3. Find a song that, for you, fits into the category of what African American leader W.E.B. DuBois called a "sorrow song." Locate a space in your home that you can make a sanctuary and listen to the song. Move to the music or allow whatever emotions emerge. Then, give yourself the gift of stillness. Take notes on whatever happens when the song or songs finish.

Chapter Twelve

Visual Arts and Architecture: Memorializing Memories

I missed the announcement of the spring opening, or maybe there wasn't one given Covid restrictions, so it took me a while to get myself to the Frick Museum to experience Vanessa German's installation, *Reckoning: Grief* and Light. I was drawn first by the artist, a Pittsburgh-based African American woman I'd met when I first came to town in 2005. We were both part of a site-specific dance performance of the Mary Miller Dance Company held in a downtown warehouse. Vanessa was featured as a spoken word artist—one of her many gifts. Now with an international reputation due to her own site-specific installations, Vanessa describes herself as a "citizen artist." She calls her work "experiments with freedom," addressing the questions our country needs to be asking in this critical time of reckoning. "How can I be whole here? How can *we* be whole here? How do *we* heal?"

The topic draws me in. As a dancing social worker and grief advocate, I know the role the arts can play to help us metabolize our grief, not only from personal losses but from large scale societal trauma and loss. As an improv artist, I appreciate the role installation art can play in connecting the dots between personal experience and societal events.

We all watched on our television screens as a Black man was being murdered by a policeman. And we've witnessed more people lose their lives since then, in the streets and in their own homes. We're grappling with our own personal and communal values. How do we heal from what we've been learning about ourselves, as a nation, as a people?

After getting some directions from a staff member, I walk softly into the darkened gallery so as not to disturb the quiet that greets me there. The reddish-brown colored walls are hung with Italian Renaissance devotional paintings. Filling one end of the room, three larger-than-life cobalt blue and gold sculptures stand, somehow at home in a room of gilded altar pieces bearing images of saints and martyrs.

I feel dwarfed by the gigantic feminine figures dressed in ruffled ball gowns made of layered blue glass bottles. A sign contains the artist's permission for visitors to experience our sorrow. "Nothing can separate you from the language you cry in." It invites me to sit on the church pew placed in front of the altar, to meditate and notice the passing of time. Vanessa's voice on a continual audio loop counts down the number of minutes that the officer's knee was on the neck of George Floyd.

I note the tiny male figure dressed in a seventeenth century uniform standing on top of a Black woman's head, swigging liquid from a raised bottle. I notice elaborately gilded birds and flowers and fruit. I recognize our national bird, the eagle, above an alarm clock–all against a backdrop of a blue cloud-filled sky. Coke bottles recall for me the song from a coke commercial years ago; "I'd love to teach the world to sing in perfect harmony."

Staying true to the multi-sensory aspect of installment art, excerpts of a musical work play in the background. The work originally debuted in 2019 by the Colour of Music

216

Festival Orchestra at Pittsburgh's Carnegie Hall. "Unburied, Unmourned, Unmarked: Requiem for Rice" by Jonathan Wineglass is based on the libretto written by Dr. Edda L. Fields-Black.

Moving closer to the installation, I see myself, literally, in the structures in front of me. Strategically placed mirrors capture the reflection of my face, and as I move away, my image disappears. Museum notes describe the cascade of blue glass as invoking a "reimagined wailing wall" or "weeping river." Just then, a couple enters the room from the adjacent gallery, taking a shortcut through this gallery to the next one. I hear the man's voice behind me say to his wife, "Look, so many medicine bottles." I hadn't seen the glass bottles as that. But then, after he mentioned it, of course they are medicine bottles. Medicine for our individual and collective healing.

Visual art is what people usually think of when they hear the word "art." Arts that are categorized as visual arts—painting, sculpture, film, drawing, ceramics, crafts, print making, photography, video, and architecture—are appreciated primarily through our sense of sight. Visual communication is more effective than words alone, hence the saying, "A picture is worth a thousand words."

As we view an art piece, characteristics of its color, size, shape, line, and its aesthetic organization (composition) attract our attention. The artist, through the arrangement of these elements, expresses themselves and communicates complex ideas, concepts, and emotions quickly, helping us develop clarity about our culture, our history, our own lives, and those of our contemporaries.

From the perspective of the purposes of art, Vanessa German's installation, *Reckoning: Grief and Light,* provides an exquisite example of how interacting with visual art can facilitate our processing of grief and loss experiences. Installation art connects our personal lives to the larger societal events that we, or our ancestors, have witnessed.

1) **Ceremonial**—It's size and dramatic color signal that it is commemorating something important in our culture and in our personal lives.

2) **Functional**— The installment is made up of found objects, many familiar but positioned or used in an unfamiliar way.

3) **Persuasive**—There is an invitation to interact with the piece, to bring our own experiences and memories into the space. Mirrors are placed so that, as a visitor, we see a reflection of our own image as we view the work. We re-experience the number of minutes that the officer's knee was on the victim's neck.

4) **Artistic expression**—Vanessa has added vocal speech, music, and suggested activity to the visual feast she has invited us to participate in. By going beyond our sense of sight to arts that enlist the visitors' auditory and kinesthetic senses, a full-bodied experience is encouraged. As the artist communicates her own point of view, she encourages us to recognize and question our own.

Art and Memories

Memories are what's left after the loss of a loved one, and our creativity and various art forms serve to create a place or an object on which to focus those memories. After my son Ken died of AIDS on the summer solstice in 1997, the year he turned thirty-one years of age, my friend Rebecca told me about an offer her horticulturist father made to families who wanted to remember a loved one. His specialty was Daylilies, the flower where each bud blooms for the length of a single day. He was continually coming up with new varieties, and if you bought a certain number of a new variety, you were given the option of naming that variety. One of Ken's art forms was flower arranging, so having a flower named after him that went home with all the members of his family across the country to bloom in subsequent springs and summers seemed a beautiful way to remind us of him. So, "Ken of Arlington" was born.

The environment that daylilies can tolerate is quite varied, but in some cases, we may have pushed the boundaries a bit too far. After the funeral, members of our far-flung family traveled home and planted this new daylily in Texas, New Mexico, Oregon, Washington State, Nebraska, Nevada, Kentucky, Michigan, and Florida. In addition to the flowers that were planted outside, Rebecca gave us a memento as a keepsake for our home—a framed photograph of "Ken of Arlington" with the quote, "When a loved one becomes a memory then the memory becomes a treasure."

The Art We Make

Psychologists have long found abstract images and drawings to be useful tools to access and understand a person's unconscious thought patterns and emotions. In the Rorschach or ink blot test, a person is shown a series of ambiguous images and asked to interpret or project onto them any meaning they might find there. Like identifying images in cloud formations, what a person sees can tell the therapist or psychologist a lot about their personality or their present state of mind. This type of process can be used by the person themselves to get in touch with their own unconscious patterns and emotions.

Therapists who work with children often ask them to

draw a picture of their family, followed by the direction, "Tell me the story of your picture." Things that become important about the drawing are who the figures represent, their size and placement on the page, and where the child places themself in the grouping. Is there someone missing from the picture? What is the spatial relationship between the figures? What other items are included: buildings, trees, sun, clouds, and what do they represent for the person making the drawing?

Michelle Baker uses her art therapy background to encourage people to move beyond the idea of art as making pretty pictures to imagining art as what she calls a "soul language." She teaches her students how to bypass the thinking mind and use her intuitive art processes to make the art that only they can make. This enables her to guide them toward healing and purpose.

As with all art forms, the first hurdle Michelle must help people overcome is the one my friend Glenda described when she and I were teaching an exploring creativity workshop at a women's prison near Austin. The workshop was designed to encourage the women to see themselves as creative and confident enough to sign up for programs being offered to inmates the following semester. We began by owning up to our own lack of confidence in ourselves. "I remember the exact moment when I decided that I was not creative," Glenda told the group. "I was six years old, and we had been asked by our first-grade teacher to draw a chicken. I drew something, and then I looked at what the girl next to me had drawn. Her drawing looked exactly like a chicken. When I looked back at what I had drawn, I decided, 'I can't draw. I'm not creative.' And I never even tried drawing from that day till last year when I got the idea that maybe I should get over myself about that."

Many years have transpired since that workshop at the prison. We convinced enough of the women to get over their notions that they weren't creative that the prison's next semester's art-based classes were filled. Glenda has been enjoying watercolor painting for many years now and I continue to take advantage of opportunities presented by my artist friends, despite the part of me that still hasn't given up on reminding me that I have no special skills at making visual art.

I had spent the evening at my artist friends' home, as another artist guided us in constructing an art piece from specimens of nature's fall bounty. As I was leaving, juggling my purse in one hand and my newly created treasure in the other, I told the art teacher, Dana, "No four-year-old has ever been as proud of herself as I am of myself right now."

As art therapists know, it wasn't just the finished product—the arrangement of the bark, the money coins from the "money tree," the pod of milkweed bursting from the center of the canvas, which we sprayed with hairspray to keep it from bursting all over my living room when I got it home—it was the process I went through to arrive at this place of pride and joy in my accomplishment. It was what I had to overcome to allow myself to even begin it.

I did not have the slightest belief that I could create something of beauty. After all, I'm not a visual artist. But as I listened to that thought in my head, it sounded a lot like what people tell me when I invite them to dance, "I'm not graceful," or sing, "I can't carry a tune," or tell a story, "I don't like to talk in front of people."

In InterPlay, where we perform expressive art, we often blame the fact that most of us have seen and heard world-class artists in all fields of art and we back away from that comparison before we begin. For encouragement, we remind ourselves that folk art, or the art of regular people, is the way communities have lived their lives together for eons, using their birthright practices of dancing, singing, telling stories, and creating beautiful and useful objects as they celebrated their lives and mourned their losses.

In thanking Dana for this opportunity, I mentioned my work around the theme of *The Art of Grieving*, and we spoke a bit about what the visual arts offer someone amid an episode of grief and loss. Beginning to create something new becomes reassuring when you are coming from a place of endings. When life has taken something from us, art-making offers a place to take charge and craft the story or the image or object the way we want it to be presented. And sometimes, it's just simply satisfying to find or create order in the middle of the messiness of life.

Accessing our creativity and following our creative impulses means we have a way into our discomfort and dis-ease, and then, when the piece is finished, the story ended, art-making provides a way out, for now. And perhaps, more insight into who we truly are.

The Art We Gift

When friends and family members experience a significant loss, *we* are at a *loss for words*. Many sympathy cards state versions of that truth. As we shuffle through the offerings at the card shop or drugstore greeting card counter, it's the images and artwork on the card that strongly affect our selection. There is a lot we want the card to express for us and we know that, at a difficult time, words can seem too simplistic or trite. They may even offend.

We want people to know that they are not alone, that we care. We want to remind them that we are here for them, that we have confidence in them. We wish that their memories will sustain them through the pain and beyond. These wishes do not only apply when someone has lost a loved one through death. Messages of love and support are sorely needed when the loss is one of a person's good health or physical abilities.

"You're not as you were," the doctor tells me as he shows me the x-ray of my shoulder. The picture means little to me since I'm not totally clear on what the shoulder bones are supposed to look like. It's been three months since my fall in my dance class, when I was moving sideways on a sticky floor and couldn't get my feet under me in time. I landed directly on my left shoulder, breaking it in a couple of places. After the doctor directs me to push against his hands and reach up overhead, he declares, "You are at eighty percent." I tell him, "I'm really not an eighty percent kind of gal," so he gives me a script for more physical therapy sessions.

The PT sessions direct the incredibly demanding work I must do to get back to my "old self" and my mission in life, which seems to be to become the world's oldest known person still dancing. What helps me stick to my challenging recovery course is an art piece created and given to me by another dancer, artist friend, and mentor Cynthia Winton-Henry. Her shoulder injury had been a couple of months before mine (her right, my left), and she was nearly back to a complete range of motion by this time, which encouraged me to believe such a thing was possible.

Her recovery program included all of what I was doing along with her spiritual practice of making art out of whatever comes into her life. We commiserated about our "broken wings," and when I saw her at the InterPlay National Conference, she gifted me an art piece she created for me out of found objects. The construction of the piece must have begun with her finding a framed painting of a Madonna figure, which helped to establish its title: *Our Lady of the Broken Wing*. There is a three-dimensional element to the blue framed shrine. A three-inch heart-shaped cushion covered with animal skin designs holds a realistic image of the human rib cage, glued to the center of the woman's chest. Green goblin figures loom across the bottom of the piece, and a monstrous blue sea creature's tentacles hang down from the upper left corner. Purple tear drops and scary grotesque fingers grip the woman's left shoulder, making it clear what must be overcome.

Cynthia is a shrine maker, a maker of sacred spaces. This shrine is to honor our brokenness, individual and collective. The images powerfully illustrate what we are up against in those times of injury and desired recovery. Hope is illustrated as well—the much-needed encouragement to keep on keeping on. The beaded jeweled swag and sparkling star-studded emblem that drape and surround the frame represent this challenge as a noble purpose, and one that will conclude in transformation. And as *Our Lady of the Broken Wing* continues to adorn the wall beside my bed, years after that transformation, she continues to remind me of the love that was infused into her by her creator, one of my dearest mentors and friends.

Communal Memorials

Visiting a communal memorial involves being taken on a journey where elements of visual art (architecture, color, symbols) and the landscaped natural world create an experience that encourages contemplation, reminiscence, and sometimes conversational processing when experienced with friends or loved ones. The structures take us into the setting, offer an experience, and bring us out. They return us to our regular lives, often changed or transformed.

In the summer of 2022, my husband and I visited our nation's capital with his two brothers and their wives, and we took some time to see the Vietnam Veterans Memorial. Walking a concrete path alongside panels of the black granite wall, we were almost overwhelmed by the size and space taken up by 57,939 service men and women's engraved names. The placement of the names and the way they cluster, fewer at the beginning, more concentrated in the middle, give us a sense of the years and progression of time and the loss of lives in what finally turned out to be a twenty-year conflict.

Moving closer to the names on the wall, our faces reflect in the mirror-like granite, making us a part of the structure and bringing us into each time frame represented. The path we walk takes us through a timeline that begins before our nation's encounter in Vietnam was an officially declared war through the fall of Saigon in the summer of 1975, when troops were airlifted out, leaving behind many South Vietnamese people who had supported us.

The walk, and our interactions with the names on the wall, take us back to that time of incredible division in our country over the war, and the time in our own lives when the young men in our families were subject to the draft. Though their father served in World War II, Rich and his brother Chuck had drawn high lottery numbers and were relieved to be able to continue in college without serving in this war. Brother Jay served in the armed forces after he became a dentist, but he was assigned to Korea, so he did not serve in what is sometimes referred to as "the theater" of the Vietnam War. My brother Kenny hung around with two friends in high school, and when all three were drafted, each of the three made different decisions regarding the war. Joe moved to Canada, and their other friend ended up driving a munitions truck on the front lines. Kenny applied for and got conscientious objector status and did alternative service in a hospital for two years during the war.

We're accompanied on our walk by dozens of people we don't know from various generations. Those wearing red jackets are veterans being pushed in wheelchairs by volunteers from a veterans' organization. One man clearly knew several people whose names were on the wall as he stopped often to find and read them. A dark-skinned man wearing a veteran cap was traversing the wall in the opposite direction. As he came towards us, he maneuvered his own wheelchair with a skill that demonstrated he'd been traveling in that apparatus for a long time. As people walking in our direction encountered him, they said, "Thank you for your service," and he responded with a broad smile. We pass a grade-school-aged girl tracing the name of a relative onto a small piece of paper with some direction from her parents. Presumably, she will take the paper home as a keepsake and remembrance of an ancestor she never got to meet.

We finish our walk, stop to catch our breath, and dry a few tears. This experience has been a catalyst to share memories of that time with one another. We each know people who served and came home, never to be the same again. In the years since, we know Vietnamese refugees or their children, now grown, who made it to this country—a friend from work, a book club member, my nail technician. We wonder what's happened to people who left our country rather than serve in what they felt was an "unjust war." The tension over the war has dissipated, and we have found other issues to disagree about as a country.

We wonder what part this memorial has played in the forty years of its existence in healing our country of the bitter divisions of that time.

Perspective

A large-scale memorial can enlighten the past and clarify what we didn't understand at the time. We never had a memorial for the 1918 pandemic, which many feel is part of why we were so ill-prepared for this recent pandemic. Getting on with the war effort of that day caused the Wilson administration to downplay the pandemic to move on to what became "The Roaring 20s" and the Great Depression.

Getting on from the Covid-19 pandemic, hopefully, we won't make the same mistake. In September 2021, near the Washington Monument, artist Suzanne Brennan Furstenberg created a temporary art installation, *In America: Remember.* She used 630,000 white flags to represent the lives that had been lost by that time. The artist described her intention: "My twenty-five years of hospice volunteering taught me every life is valuable, no death is just a statistic." Hearing statistics doesn't make it real but seeing the fields of individual flags blowing in the breeze, we begin to appreciate the extent of the human losses we have suffered individually and as a nation.

Memorials can help us fashion a different future by being clear about what has happened that we need to understand better and never forget. This effort is clear as a step in righting a wrong, as happens in The National Memorial for Peace and Justice (also known as The Lynching Memorial). It uses art and sculpture to help us confront one of the darkest elements of our collective past. It features samples of earth collected at sites where lynching occurred, and encourages people to research their own communities, add to the museum's collection, and mark by signage in their own communities what is now sacred ground.

Art to Transform Place

In places where atrocities have been committed, the space itself must be transformed, sometimes by members of the community who live there. We can learn a great deal about how art can transform grief through the work of community building artist Lily Yeh. She finds "an organic process that naturally occurs when creativity is introduced into broken places." This happens when the process is "open and inclusive, and the goal is for the common good." Yeh has traveled to and consulted with communities in many broken places in the world, including Rwanda, China, Ecuador, Haiti, Ghana, Syria, Italy, and the U.S. "The world is full of darkness," Yeh says and, "Beauty is intimately engaged with darkness and destruction. Art brings color and light so you can walk into the darkness and hold it in your arms."

Yeh's work, which she describes in her 2013 TEDx talk involves consulting with community members, encouraging them to envision what they want the desecrated space to now covey, and what wounds they want to heal as they honor the lives that were lost.

In the 2014 film *The Barefoot Artist*, we see how Yeh helps individuals and communities to move from brokenness to wholeness. We also see how she uses her own version of art as therapy to atone for her father's life by connecting with her half siblings he walked away from before she was born, when he became an American immigrant.

Other redesigns of place and space are the 9/11 Memorial in New York City and the Flight 93 site in Shanksville, Pennsylvania. After consultation with those who lost loved ones in the terrorist attack, the cavern created by the fall of the towers is now a reflecting pool, with the nearly three-thousand names of people that were lost inscribed on the bronze ledge that surrounds the water that continually disappears into the deep center. Landscaping artists created a serene park-like setting, and every year on the anniversary, in a ceremony on the site, the names of the fallen are read aloud by family members of the deceased.

The Flight 93 memorial site a vacant meadow in Pennsylvania, where mutinous passengers diverted the plane from its path to the Capital, forcing it to crash there. Architects consulted with loved ones of those on the plane and with citizens on the ground in nearby communities to develop it. A building was constructed that offers a place for visitors to stand and experience the angle of descent of the plane as it came down, viewing the part of the meadow that has now became holy ground. Other elements include a tower of voices and a wall of names that leads to the field that contains the remains of the plane and the forty-four passengers who perished in it. The visitor center encourages people to interact with the story of how the passengers attempted to get control of the plane from the hijackers, and what their brave actions have meant throughout the years since.

Healing the Culture

Art can call attention to a cultural problem or injustice in such a way that it makes an emotional impact, inspiring people to act to change the unfortunate circumstances that created it. Those unfortunate situations may have historical roots in the histories of our own ancestors, making it necessary to have honest conversations with the youngest members of our own families. Such conversations were stimulated by a trip I made with family members and a friend to the site of a healing art installation on a native reservation in the Morongo Valley desert near Palm Springs, California.

My nine-year-old granddaughter Kyra, who is Native American, my best friend Pam from Pittsburgh, and I were traveling in a green bug of a car, creeping slowly over an uneven sandy, rocky trail of a road, hoping to avoid damage and a fine from the car rental company. We were headed to the studio and home of Native American artist Sharon Davis to view her art installations and memorials. "Just keep heading toward the mountain. I'm the last house on the road," Sharon said, so we keep on, slowly swerving around rocks and cautiously traversing dips and elevations in the path before us.

"I heard people sometimes approach a sacred site on their knees, '' Pam says.

"Well, this is our version of that practice," I say.

It's not hard to recognize when we've made it to the right place. Amidst the desert's canvas of many shades of beige and brown, colorful visual stimulation appears. The cottage and transformed former garage are coated with navy blue paint and colorful graphics. Sharon emerges to greet us, herself an art piece, dressed in black tights and a shirt containing the letters *Warrior Mother.* (Hmm, quite a coincidence I think.) Her straight bright red hair sparkles in the sunlight. We see her sense of humor immediately as she begins to walk us around her property. Serving as our guide, she points to a collection of objects; bicycle wheels, a paint can, wood, and metal tubing, arranged by her artist's eye and tied together to create a purple sculpture. "These are items I found on my property when I moved here." Taking what others left when they disrespect the land, Sharon uses and makes art out of them. Next, we pause at an arrangement of glass objects she calls "Crystal Cactus," which are mixed in with real cacti, one in full bloom.

We pause next at a sign that contains a drawing of a pair of small moccasins and the numbers "215" beside the words, "We were children." Two hundred and fifteen pieces of hair twisted and tied with orange ribbons hang together, positioned over a pair of adult size white boots. They represent the children that did not live long enough to wear them. They are part of the more than one-thousand missing and murdered native women and children in North America

230

that Sharon's art installations seek to gain public recognition for. As Sharon speaks of these atrocities, I look over at my nine-year-old Native American granddaughter and wonder to myself, "Is it okay that I brought her here?"

We move our focus to the red dresses hanging on clotheslines, each dress blowing independently at various rhythms as the wind swirls around them. We experience the women's presence, in this marking of the absence of their bodies to fill the dresses.

In the quiet, yet powerfully loud social commentary, I hear a protest and remember the wisdom of grief expert, Francis Weller, who suggests, "Part of the medicine we need right now is to come out of the fiction that grief is individual." Or to imagine that grief ends with the generation that first experienced the loss. "If the sequestered grief that surrounds us made a sound, the whole world would be weeping." And the sorrow I feel inhabits my whole body and grounds my feet to the desert floor.

Sharon describes the ceremonies the women do when they change the dresses out. The desert sun takes the color out of them quickly, and they need to be replaced often. With drums and chanting and the stomping steps of their dancing feet, they crumble the dresses and throw them to the ground so, as they disintegrate, they become part of the earth. We promise to join women from near and far who watch for red dresses in resale shops and send them to Sharon to keep her art installation going.

Before I leave California, Pam and I have several conversations about what Kyra does not yet know about the mistreatment and attempted genocide of her Native American ancestors. And the fact that other ancestors were likely on the other side of these atrocities. We admit that we don't know how to talk about those dark topics with her. But we see this experience as having at least opened the door to such efforts. We were successful in finding several red dresses in Kyra's favorite resale store. We purchased and dropped them off at the art center for Sharon to use as replacements for the ones now blowing in the desert sun.

Objects That Help Us Remember

Not all memorials need to be grandiose in size to be effective. On a smaller scale, we can build memorials that serve our personal and family needs, whether it's framing photos, creating a slideshow, planting a tree, or assembling items on a shelf that remind us of who and what we have lost, so we can keep enduring connections with them.

A simple cement sculpture of two young girls, one of them taller with a ponytail, who seems to be sheltering the smaller girl, looks back at me from the small garden area outside my writing studio. My younger sister, Pat, gave it to me many years ago, long before her illness and death from Alzheimer's. When she first found it, she told me it represented for her our relationship growing up together. Now it holds the memories of our long life together, even to our last "Thelma and Louise" road trip when I broke her out of her assisted living facility near Boston for a great adventure.

Simple makeshift memorials become artistic expressions of grief that send a message. The photos, flowers, and other memorabilia we see displayed on the side of the road mark the site of an accident in such a way as to honor the person who died there while warning others of potential danger. More elaborate memorials amplify their message with longer-lasting effect. But however elaborate or simple, it's our love and appreciation for what was lost that fuels this need to express our grief with objects and their arrangement, and the arts help us create ways to experience and remember, changing us and our world for the better.

Finding Purpose in Co-Destiny

A healthy response to the loss of a loved one through acts of violence or injustice is to act in their name to change the larger society or culture so that other families will not suffer the same fate. This is most relevant when it comes to the issue of gun violence in schools. We must never forget the Sandy Hook elementary school shooting in Newtown, Massachusetts on December 14, 2012, when a twenty-year-old former student shot and killed his mother and then entered the school and killed twenty six and seven-year-olds and six adult staff members before turning the gun on himself. An investigation concluded that the shooter's mental state and access to lethal weapons was the cause of the event.

Since the extent of this atrocity had been so egregious, the hope was that now, finally, something could be done to keep guns out of the hands of people who should not have them. The grieving parents and community members of Newtown organized the Newtown Action Alliance Foundation to #EndGunViolence in America. They also sued the gun manufacturer, Remington Arms, and settled for $73 million dollars.

It took nearly ten years for a Newtown memorial to be designed, built, and opened to the public. The memorial made the Wall Street Journal's list of Best Architecture of 2022, offering a way to measure its value: "It would be wrong to judge the heartbreaking Sandy Hook Permanent Memorial on any criterion but this one: does it offer solace and healing to those whose family and friends were among the twenty-six

233

victims of the infamous mass shooting?"

Newtown developed a tradition of marking anniversaries of the shooting with quiet reflection, so for the memorial, there was no opening ceremony. The aerial view of the memorial highlights its spiral design and the prominence of a tree in the center of a circular space in a clearing near the rebuilt school. The walkway appears to be spiraling down, and the names of the dead are engraved in stone surrounding the pond. Another image shows wreaths with candles floating counterclockwise in the water.

Words from a speech President Barack Obama made at a vigil two days after the incident are included on a plaque: "Here in Newtown, I come to offer the love and prayers of a nation. I am very mindful that mere words cannot match the depths of your sorrow, nor can they heal your wounded hearts. I can only hope it helps for you to know that you're not alone in your grief; that our world, too, has been torn apart; that all across this land of ours, we have wept with you."

Not everyone has been weeping with the survivors. The Sandy Hook massacre has become a catalyst for societal change, which gun advocates are continuing to resist. This quiet space keeps its head down with few signs and a small parking lot so as not to be interrupted by gun advocates who have made false claims that the Sandy Hook massacre was a hoax designed to promote gun control.

It's hard to imagine a more hostile attack on the surviving family and community members' right to grieve. Psychologists would call this outright lie and manipulation of reality "gaslighting," and like the holocaust deniers, their aim is to manipulate people into questioning their own memories, their own sanity. By offering an alternative version of history and reality, they hope to undermine the efforts survivors and their supporters are making to ensure that such atrocities cease.

Since the road to such a future is turning out to be a lot longer than expected, the memorial will need to offer the community a collective sigh of grief and a place of solace and comfort for years to come. *The Wall Street Journal* architectural reviewer, Michael J Lewis, offered the following story, illustrative of the effect on him of his visit:

> "I visited it at dusk during a chilly November rain and watched the only other visitor carefully place a stone on one of the names. He told me it was for one of the victims, a newly hired teaching assistant who had just gotten her 'dream job.' The dignity of this simple gesture, performed under the bleakest of New England skies suggests that at least one creation of 2022 got it exactly right."

Resource for Art as Therapy

Art therapy is a mental health profession that enriches the lives of individuals, families, and communities through active art-making, creative process, applied psychological theory, and human experiences within a psychotherapeutic relationship. Learn more at https://arttherapy.org/about/

Reflection/Action

1. View one of the memorials described in this chapter online. Notice how viewing it on the screen affects your feelings and attitudes about the event or circumstance it honors or represents. If you have already visited one of the memorials featured in this chapter in person, check it out online. See if

you learn anything more about the theme on which it is based to add to what you experienced in person.

2. Visit an art installation at a local art gallery or community center. See if any of the pieces connect to the theme of grief and loss and/or to your own grief experiences. Journal about its effect on your thoughts and feelings.

3. Michelle Baker's Art as a Soul Language® site and learn more about how drawing simple stick figures can reveal to you inner truths about yourself. As she puts it, "Art is the language of your soul. It's time to listen to what it's telling you."

Part IV
Transformation: Deepening

"Oh, earth, you're too wonderful for anybody to realize you. Do any human beings ever realize life while they live it—every, every minute?"

-Thornton Wilder, Our Town

Chapter Thirteen

Curating Our Experiences
Towards an Artful Life

Years ago, after my friend Jyoti King was diagnosed with Alzheimer's, and before its cruel ravages had begun, she gave me a treasure box as a gift for my birthday. The box is 10 x 10 square inches, made of brown polished wood and lined inside to be a receptacle for objects, perhaps jewelry or other keepsake items. The cover is decorated with a copper metal medallion surrounded by a narrow strip of purple suede, inscribed with a quote from Maya Angelou, "Your *life* is more *important* than you think. It's your first *treasure.*"

I loved the box and her generosity in gifting it to me, but I wasn't sure I had anything valuable enough that warranted such a box to keep in it. Yet, the quote was saying that it was *my life itself* that was the treasure. I finally have gotten old enough, mature enough, or close enough to my own life's end that I'm beginning to understand Maya Angelou (and Jyoti's) point.

As the life experiences of our gains and losses unfold, leaving their mark of memories on our bodies, minds, and spirits, the changing levels of the grief spiral, as it moves through the seasons of our years, offers opportunities for new perspectives and to reflect on and process them. Some of these experiences we have sought out, others we have had little choice about, but what matters is our reactions, what we make of our experiences, and what these experiences make of us.

The arts of music, dance, painting, sculpture, drama, literature, when done on our behalf, take us into liminal space, that "space between the worlds," where such processing takes place. The art we make comes out of what happens to us and transforms us into our intuitive mind, what Einstein calls "the sacred gift," to which, counterculturally, he believes "the rational mind" should be its "faithful servant."

In revisiting the box to describe it more vividly, I found a copy of a poem I had written and given to members of my improv troupe to thank them for participating with me in a 2010 TEDx talk. It wanted to be shared: –

The Pearl

It begins like many of life's challenges,
with a random, seemingly insignificant
incident. A single grain of sand intrudes,
and becomes an unwanted guest.

Creative, concentric life processes are
pressed into play, stimulating the organism
to weave and wrap a smooth, protective
coating around the offending particle.

Mother Nature, grappling with her
assignment, produces a lustrous

spherical structure, known throughout
the world as a valuable gem.

But the true beauty of this creation doesn't
emerge until it links with others like itself,
becoming a luminous chain, reminding us
that it is not the challenge that matters,
but the creative connections we make.

Rabbi Abraham Hershel suggests that "the meaning of life is to live life as if it were a work of art." I would add, a work of art that is continually evolving, always in process, and frequently bombarded with unexpected elements. There are people and events to integrate into our life's visual, auditory, and kinesthetic reality. Meaning and purpose come from grieving experiences of loss when, using the arts, we spend time in liminal space. We make art out of what happens to us and use the arts to express, create, and celebrate.

I hope by now, in your journey through this book, that you have become convinced that opportunities to grieve have occurred and will continue to occur throughout your life. While considering grieving itself an art, you can get good at it and have a satifying life. On the spiral path that grief and loss take, new episodes of grief and loss may harken back to previous ones. These previous losses, viewed from the new perspective the grief spiral provides, will become resources of wisdom for your future life and for the person we are becoming. And most importantly the arts can be the portal or vehicle to achieve this transformation and alchemy.

In using the arts and art-making as tools to meet the challenges our lives will undoubtably continually hand us, we must let go of the need to be exceptionally skilled or talented at any and all art. Music, dance, poetry, design, storytelling, journaling, photography, however performed or executed, have the power to change our brains from depression to joy, from uncertainty to clarity, from a sense of isolation to connection, from sorrow to hope and inspiration.

Borrowing a concept from museum curators, we structure our lives in such a way as to honor what's most important to us, selectively sharing our stories and making meaning, connecting with others to celebrate life and the gifts we receive from one another. We use the arts to express our pain, and companion others as they bear and express their own. When an episode of grief ends, we can decide what we keep as tokens of remembrance and what we let go of as no longer needed. These actions will determine who we become, and when we leave, what remains.

In the early to mid-nineties, when my youngest son Kenneth was living with AIDs, and I was in the role of his primary supporter, I had a personal physician who offered a unique perspective by consciously using the arts as part of her healing medicine. An appointment with Dr. Mary Anne began with her listening attentively as I reported my symptoms and updated her on how things were going with my son's health journey. She examined me, and after I exchanged the patient gown for my street clothes, we finished the session in her office.

After a brief discussion, she reached for her pen and wrote something on her prescription pad. She might recommend a pharmaceutical or an increase in a vitamin, a reference to a study she'd come across that might be relevant to my son's treatment, but most often she included an assignment to read a particular book or view a particular television show or movie.

Before she went to medical school, Dr. Mary

Anne had been a nun and I always thought these last "homework"assignments were good habits left over from her life as an educator. I now know her to be a generation or so ahead of her time in her expectation that art and art-based experiences can improve the quality of life, assist a person as they grieve, improve their mental health, lessen their pain, and more. Now, thirty plus years later, neuroimaging is providing to the new field of neuroaesthetics evidence that the arts transform.

In curating art tools into the grieving of our lives, it's good to revisit some truths we've discovered or rediscovered on our journey through the art of grieving.

Loss is common and frequent in most every life, and the need to grieve begins with loss. As we learned during the pandemic, losses come not only in personal situations of our own choosing; many are provided by history and fate.¬ Large scale events across the globe impact our lives, and added to our personal losses, can overwhelm our capacity to grieve and process it all. The emotions of grief can begin long before a loss arrives, inspired by our anticipation of it. So, grieving itself is an art, and one that we need to get good at in order to have a productive and satisfying life.

Western culture's rules have made grieving more difficult as they demand that we "keep calm and carry on," and whatever we do, "don't get emotional," (at least in public). Grieving requires us to experience the pain as we move through grief yet, in our there-must-be- a-pill-for-that world, we're encouraged to avoid pain, which is often the biggest barrier to grieving well.

Even what we use to think we knew about grief is no longer so. Freud recommended complete detachment from a deceased loved one while more recent science confirms mourners do better when continuing relationship bonds with their deceased loved one throughout the years of their lives. In cultures that honor their ancestors rather than seeing

243

grieving as an individual problem to be solved, the individual is supported to see themselves as part of the web of life. In ceremonies that use the arts of dance, music, and storytelling, the mourners experience their relationship to "All That Is," to "All Our Relations," and to life's larger story.

To curate the arts into your life as part of processing grief, select, arrange, and organize those arts that are most accessible and meaningful to you. To help with that, let's review the superpowers of some of the many arts:

- We are wired for story, and **storytelling** connects people to one another. It offers opportunities to frame and reframe experiences, and to companion one another on our life journeys.
- **Journal writing** provides opportunities to explore and vent thoughts and emotions privately and review them later. **Public writing,** such as letters to the editor or public essays, are ways to change the world on behalf of a loved one–an action of co-destiny, related to how they lived or died.
- **Dance** engages a sense of energy and power. As my teachers taught me, "Dance doesn't take energy, it makes energy." Movement expressed and witnessed communicates much of what there are no words for and facilitates the dancers' and witnesses' body awareness and ability to come into full presence and connection.
- **Music,** instrumental or voice, can transport us to the past, lift our spirits in the present, and help us find resolution in an episode of grief, soothing our troubled souls.
- **Visual art** stimulates the brain in areas associated with pleasure, memory, and emotion. It helps us connect unrelated items, notice novel patterns, and see things in a different light.

So, in curating the art of grieving into the work of art that is our lives, we begin as a playwright might begin, with the end in mind. From the perspective of the art of grieving, death is the north star. How do we want our story to have unfolded when we come to its eventual end? What expressions of art can match the throughline that one of my mentors, Victoria LaBalme, calls "the hidden current" of deep values and desire that carry us through? One way to identify these core values is to fast forward to the end. When you are an ancestor, what would you like your legacy to be?

If you're an elder or have reached middle age, you no doubt have had many reminders of your impermanence—experiences of illness and injury, losses of loved ones, deep disappointments, and dreams lost or deferred. But like me, you may have only recently begun to see awareness of death as a gift. Research confirms that keeping an awareness of the fact that life in this body, on this earth, will end gives added meaning to the time we are here. Hopefully, with all that fate and history have provided, most of us can say, on most days, that to be alive is a grand thing.

One way to help answer some of the above questions is to imagine your own funeral or memorial service and write your own eulogy. Researching for this assignment might lead you to photographic images on your phone, or to albums and scrapbooks in closets or storage facilities, to songs on your favorite playlists, to notecards saved from friends and loved ones through the years—in other words, to some of the art that holds your memories.

The gifts of grieving are compassion for other people and for ourselves, often accompanied by a desire to lessen suffering. I was inspired to write this book after realizing that what our society teaches about grief causes suffering and prevents people from receiving the life-long benefits of grieving well. Another gift of grieving is one of life's richest intimacies—connecting with others traversing the grief spiral alongside of us while avoiding the sense of loneliness that has become a number one health problem in our country. Gratitude for life itself is another gift of grieving, and this often leads to the gift of purpose. What do we want to do with the years of life given to us, however long or short those years turn out to be?

For the Young

In this journey of exploration about grief and how the arts can help us to traverse it, I have been encouraged by what some contemporary parents are teaching their children. Finding the tiny memorial site in my neighborhood dedicated to "the best fish in the world" brought a smile to my face and reminded me that a young child's first encounter with death is likely the loss of a pet. What a teaching moment it is for parents to support the young mourner's grief with art and a ceremony of gratitude for the life they shared.

The wisdom that children have to offer the rest of us surprised and delighted me as well. For children whose needs for safety and health have been met, the arts are a joyful playground. Dancing, drawing, singing, making objects, enacting scenarios–these are the actions that develop their creativity and create the child, encouraging them to become their authentic selves. For adults lucky enough to have opportunities to join children in this artful play, they take us back to a time when we were less inhibited, before we "knew" that we weren't creative or artistically skilled.

My granddaughter Kyra's bracelet-making for a friend

whose hamster died showed wisdom that seems to have escaped many adults. The bracelet holds a memory that can be accessed—"I can be with you whenever you think of me," the note from the hamster read. Since many children already use the arts to process and transform their lives, one of our jobs as their teachers and caregivers is to protect and encourage that to continue, perhaps providing a model for us to emulate as well.

It is said that we must first imagine the world we wish to live in before we can become a part of creating it. For me, acts of creative imagination have helped me to recognize when the art of grieving is being practiced and demonstrated. Such was the Commemoration Ceremony on the fifth anniversary of a gunman storming the Tree of Life Synagogue in Pittsburgh, killing eleven people and injuring six- the worst attack on Jews in the history of the U.S.

In the intervening years, the Pittsburgh community has done much to become "stronger than hate" the slogan that emerged early in the community's healing process. Immediately, the larger community rallied around the traumatized Jewish community, holding candlelight vigils in the streets of "Mr. Rogers' Neighborhood" where the horrific event took place. The following Friday, as Jewish people in the greater Pittsburgh area entered their temples and synagogues for Shabbat services, the pathways from their parking lots to the front doors were lined with scores of non-Jewish neighbors holding lighted candles, offering solidarity, standing in silent support.

During the first month, I was able to join other local mental health professionals to volunteer and assist persons impacted directly by the event. As happens in companioning, our own grieving processes were impacted as we offered Critical Incident Stress Debriefings for other community members at the Jewish Community Center. People who had dealt with mass shootings in their own communities visited Pittsburgh to offer support. Local leaders met with staff from resiliency centers around the country to gather lessons learned and best practices for community support. This led to the creation of the 10.27 Healing Partnership, which is continuing to provide resources and support years after the massacre. In partnership with many community agencies, opportunities for commemoration and commemorative volunteering are continuing to be provided.

It's a pleasantly warm autumn afternoon in Pittsburgh. As we walk up the hill in the park leading to where the ceremony will take place, children from nearby schools, some in their uniforms, greet us and thank us for coming. They invite us to come closer to a table that contains their artwork, colorful collage-like sculptures, each honoring one of the eleven people whose lives were taken on this day five years ago. Trilling harp strings accompany us to our seats in front of the sheltered platform that will be the stage.

As leaves flutter gently down from nearby trees, friends and family members share stories of their deceased loved ones before an audience of several hundred community members, media cameras, the governor, mayor, and county officials. Musicians play restored string instruments from the Violins of Hope, an exhibition of instruments played by Jewish musicians before and during the holocaust.

The message, communicated through the rhythmic tones of the music, is one we are all living: how the human spirit can overcome even the most daunting of circumstances. Three politicians alternate offering their prayers for our country. A rabbi and a Christian minister take turns reading stanzas of a poem by Judy Chicago titled *Merger*:

And then all that has divided us will merge.
And then compassion will be wedded to power.
And then softness will come to a world that is harsh and unkind.
And then both men and women will be gentle.
And then both women and men will be strong.
And then no person will be subject to another's will.

And then all will be rich and free and varied.
And then the greed of some will give way to the needs of many.

And then all will share equally in the Earth's abundance.

And then all will care for the sick and the weak and the old.

And then all will nourish the young.
And then all will cherish life's creatures.

And then everywhere will be called Eden once again.

Exiting the ritual space, I think about how we all share the challenges that history and fate have arranged, yet each life has specific losses and specific gifts of grace. These are the raw materials from which we fashion our individual and collective lives. For certain events, some of us are at ground zero, for others we are on the sidelines, affected less intensely.

Like the artist who creates her art through the arrangement of found objects, we come together to make art out of what happens to us and meanings from the processing of memories and their arrangement. Being there for one another, remembering together what we've lost, and honoring the path it has placed us on, we live satisfying lives, and create for the future structures and societal forms that feed our creative spirits and lay the groundwork for the creative futures of those yet to come.

Resources

Introduction

Collins, Sheila K. *Warrior Mother: Fierce Love, Unbearable Loss and Rituals that Heal*, She Writes Press, Phoenix, AZ 2013.

Wing It Performance Ensemble is an improvisational company co-founded by Phil Porter and Cynthia Winton-Henry in 1989. The players used InterPlay, a system of practices and tools to unlock the wisdom of the body and build community. https://interplay.org/ https://www.youtube.com/watch?v=AwKXcbFkOYs

Center for Disease Control, Basic Information on Breast Cancer. https://www.cdc.gov/cancer/breast/basic_info/index.htm

Sacred Dance Guild – A spiritually diverse international non-profit organization that advocates for dance as a sacred art and promotes dance as a means of spiritual growth and integrating of mind, body, and spirit with inclusivity, diversity, equity, and access as underlying principles. https://sacreddanceguild.org/about/contact/.

Dass, R., *Be Here Now*, Lama Foundation, San Cristobal, NM 1971. Helped popularize Eastern spirituality and yoga in the West.

Magsamen, S, Ross, I., *Your Brain on Art: How the Arts Transform Us*, Penguin RandomHouse, NY, NY 2023.

Lewis, C.S. (aka N.W. Clerk) *A Grief Observed*, Faber and Faber, London, UK 1961.

1: The Many Faces of Loss

Powell, J.H. *Covid 19 and the Economy.* Federal Reserve. https://www.federalreserve.gov/newsevents/speech/powell20200409a.htm.

Freleng, S. (Director) *We did it before, and we can do it again, The Fifth Column Mouse* https://www.youtube.com/watch?v=Wy5maENuo3Q.

Alexie, S. *The Absolutely True Diary of a Part-Time Indian,* Little Brown, NY, NY 2007

Bengson, A. and Bengson, S, *"The Keep Going Song,"* https://www.bengsons.com/

Bengson, A. and Bengson, S, *"My Joy is Heavy,"* https://www.bengsons.com/

Bengson, A. and Bengson, S, *When the Party's Over,* https://www.bengsons.com/

Haley, E. and Williams, L. *What's Your Grief? Lists to Help You Through Any Loss,* Quirk Books, Philadelphia, PA 2022.

2: Navigating the Grief Spiral

Lewis, C.S. (AKA N.W.Clerk) *A Grief Observed,* Faber and Faber, London, U.K.1961.

Ward, G. *Spirals: The Pattern of Existence,* Green Magic, 2006.

Newgrange World Heritage Site: https://www.newgrange.com/.

O'Connor, M.F., *The Grieving Brain: The Surprising Science of How We Learn from Love and Loss,* Harper Collins Publishers NY, NY 2023.

Didion, J., *The Year of Magical Thinking,* Knopf, NY, NY 2005.

The Great Wave of Kanagawa, Japanese woodblock print, MOA Museum of Art, https://www.metmuseum.org/art/collection/search/45434.

Bolte-Taylor, J., *My Stroke of Insight: A Brain Scientist's Personal Journey,* Viking, NY, NY 2008.

The Labyrinth Society History and Walking: https://www.youtube.com/
watch?v=o7u8oZLEh3M.

Winton-Henry, C. Shrine Artist, https://www.facebook.com/
ShrineWorkshop/.

Winton-Henry, C. *The Art of Ensoulment: A Playbook on How to Create from Body and Soul.* Platypus, Press, Austin, TX, 2023.

3: Culture and Emotions: The Water We Swim In

Kubler-Ross, E., *On Death and Dying,* Macmillan Company, NY, NY 1969.

Freud, S., *On Mourning and Melancholia,* Penguin Modern Classics, London, UK 2005.

Bokanowski, T., *On Freud's "Mourning and Melancholia,"* The International Psychoanalytical Association, Contemporary Freud Turning Points and Critical Issues Series, 1st Edition, Routledge, N Y, NY 2019.

Edelman, H. *Pandemic Grief Could Become Its Own Health Crisis.* Washington Post Op-Ed February 26, 2021. https://www.washingtonpost.com/
opinions/2021/02/26/pandemic-grief-could-become-its-
own-health-crisis/

Brown, B., *Atlas of the Heart: Mapping Meaningful Connection and the Language of Human Experience,* Random House, 2021.

Haley, E Williams, L., A Concept You Should Care About: Continuing Bonds, *What's Your Grief?* https://whatsyourgrief.com/
grief-concept-care-continuing-bonds.

The Guardian, *Mark Twain manuscript reveals the author's pain at losing his daughter,* Guardian, 2010, https://www.theguardian.com/
books/2010/apr/21/mark-twain-manuscript-daughter-susy

Kim-Kort, M, *I'm a Scholar of Religion. Here is What I See in the Atlanta Shootings* Op-Ed New York Times, March 28, 2021 https://www.nytimes.com/2021/03/24/opinion/atlanta-shootings-women-religion.html?searchResultPosition=1.

Dass, R., *Walking Each Other Home*, Sounds True, Louisville, CO 2018

InterPlay/Body Wisdom Inc. is an international, non-profit organization that manages the intellectual property of the art-based system known as InterPlay. Body Wisdom is responsible for teaching, training, and certifying teachers and leaders in using InterPlay, an active, creative, approach to unlocking the wisdom of the body. The InterPlay practice is used in education at all levels, creative arts, social work and therapies, and religious and spiritual communities. Interplay is located in 60 cities in the US and Australia, India, Africa, England, Germany, Scotland, and the Netherlands. https://www.interplay.org/

Inside Out is an American animated coming-of-age film released by Pixar in 2015. https://www.youtube.com/watch?v=yRUAzGQ3nSY

4: The Arts as Grief's Collaborator

Louisville Fund for the Arts, One of the country's two oldest United Arts Funds, was founded in 1949 in Louisville, KY. The organization supports, promotes, and develops arts, artists, and art organizations to create a healthy and vibrant community. https://fundforthearts.org/.

Faulkner, W. Banquet Speech: Nobel Prize for Literature. December, 1950. https://www.nobelprize.org/prizes/literature/1949/faulkner/speech/.

Maraviglia, M. *About Art: What Do We Really Mean?* Smash Magazine. July, 2010. https://www.smashingmagazine.com/2010/07/what-do-we-really-mean-by-art/.

Magsamen, S.R., *Your Brain on Art: How the Arts Transform Us*, Penguin Random House, NY, NY 2023.

Langer, S.K., *Feeling and Form*, Macmillan Publishing, NY, NY 1953.

The Grief Deck, A project of the Artists' Literacies Institute and Adriene
  Jenik, was made possible by The Ohio Hospice/National
  Hospice Cooperative, Daniel Abary, and the artists and
  grief workers who contributed their talent and wisdom
  and Kickstarter donors. https://griefdeck.com/

5: Sweet Sorrow Through the Long Arc
of Grieving

The Sankofa Bird Liberty African American Legacy Memorial:
  https://www.libertylegacymemorial.org/sankofabird Page 232

Doka, K. *Living with a Life-Threatening Illness.* Jossey-Bass, NNY, NY 1998

Gendler, J.R. *The Book of Qualities.* Harper Perennial, NY, NY 1988

Walker, B.G. *The Women's Encyclopedia of Myths and Secrets.* Harper One,
  NY, NY 1983

Wimmin, C. song, *"Kinder,"* from the album, "The Right to Be Here."

Reimagine is an organization that began in 2016 by sponsoring festivals to
  investigate the intersection of art, community, and end-of-
  life. In response to the pandemic, we began hosting community-
  driven experiences online – to help all people face adversity, loss,
  and mortality and channel the hard parts of life into meaningful
  action and growth. https://letsreimagine.org/

Phoenix, S., song artist: https://phoenixsongmusic.com/

Co-Destiny is the notion that if a person does good in the name of a deceased
loved one, it adds to that person's legacy. Joseph E Casper is a physician
and breaved parent whose son died as a teenager. His Masters in Applied
Positive Psychology was obtained at the University of Pennsylvania in 2013
partly through a capstone project where he proposed a post-traumatic
growth model for parental bereavement.

Edelman, H., *The After Grief: Finding Your Way Along the Long Arc of Loss,*
  Ballantine Books, NY. 2020

6: Illness, Aging, Disabilities, Diminishments: Good Will Come from This

Clarkson, K. Song- "Stronger." 2011, https://www.youtube.com/watch?v=Xn676-fLq7I

Feldenkrais, M., Awareness Through Movement, https://feldenkrais.com/about-the-feldenkrais-method/

Siegel, B.S.., *Love, Medicine and Miracles: Lessons Learned about Self-Healing From a Surgeons Experience with Exceptional Patients,* initially published in 1984, Harper Perennial, NY, NY 1988

Rohr, R. *A Deeper Lightness, Falling Upward: The Second Half of Life,* Center for Action and Contemplation, https://cac.org/daily-meditations/a-deeper-lightness/ November 15, 2023

Feiffer, J., an American cartoonist and author, considered the most widely read satirist in the country: https://www.google.com/search?client=firefox-b-1-d&q=jules+Feiffer

Jaquad, S. The Isolation Journals, Transforming life's interruptions into creative grist: https://theisolationjournals.substack.com/

7: Estrangement: Broken Hearts, Families, and Careers

Pellemer, K. *Fault Lines: Fractured Families and How to Mend Them,* Avery, NY, NY 2020..

Agllias, K., *Family Estrangement: A Matter of Perspective,* Routledge, NY, NY 2016.

Sedeka, N. Song- *Breaking Up is Hard to Do:* https://www.youtube.com/watch?v=KNoy3x9Yj58

Swift, T. Song- *You Belong with Me:* https://www.youtube.com/watch?v=BOZEj8wyj-I

Turner, T. Song- *What's Love Got to Do with It?*: https://www.youtube.com/watch?v=oGpFcHTxjZs

Cyrus, M. Song *Flowers:* https://www.youtube.com/watch?v=G7KNmW9a75Y

Association for Play Therapy: Mental Health Professionals Applying the Therapeutic Power of Play, https://www.a4pt.org/

Eilish, B, Song- Performed by The Bengsons, *When the Party's Over:* https://bit.ly/3UHUIZA.

8 Death: Celebrating Life and Love to the End

Smith, J.Y. *William Saroyan Dies at 72.* Washington Post, https://bit.ly/3UHUIZA.

Magussen, M., *The Gentle Art of Swedish Death Cleaning,* Scribner, NY, NY 2018.

LeBaron, M., *Transforming Death: Creating Sacred Space for the Dying,* Self-published, 2020.

Bergwall, H., Co-founder of the *WeCroak App,* host of the *WeCroak Podcast.* He ghostwrites for death in the *Ask Death Advice Column.* https://www.wecroak.com/team1.

Oliver, M. *In Blackwater Woods.* American Primitive. Back Bay Books, Boston, MA 1983.

Schels, W. and Lakotta, B. photography exhibit, *Life Before Death.* Notre-Dame- des-Neiges, 2012 https://cvltnation.com/life-before-death-walter-schels-portraits-of-people-before-and-after-death/.

Hafiz. *The Collected Poems of Hafiz.* Translated by John Payne. Digireads.com, Overland Park, KS 2011.

Taylor, Glenda, One and All Wisdom, https://oneandallwisdom.com/
author/glenda/.

Threshold Choir, Songs of Comfort to the Dying, https://thresholdchoir.
org/ contains a world map that shows pins for locations in North
America, Europe, Australia, and South Africa.

Wolfelt, Alan D., a death educator and grief counselor, is founder
and director of the Center for Loss and Life Transition, https://
www.centerforloss.com/.

Lawrence, L., *God Danced the day you were born*,
https://www.youtube.com/watch?v=XhAaOeypmsU/.

Video of the song" My Joy is Heavy! The Bengsons.
https://www.youtube.com/watch?v=kMTBaFm5ibc/.

Palidofsky, J., Hospice chaplain, musician, *"Life Me Up,"* song from
the album *Dancing Toward the Light.* https://www.youtube.com/
watch?v=iKZg7zsqzLo

9: Storytelling: Making Meaning and Sharing Truth

Andrews, E.J., *Living Revision: A Writer's Craft as Spiritual Practice*, Skinner
House Books, Boston, MA 2018.

Cameron, J., *"The Artist Way, A Spiritual Path to Higher Creativity,* Tarcher,
NY, NY 1992.

Pennebaker, J. (1997) W. Writing About Emotional Experiences as a
Therapeutic Process, *Psychological Science* 8, 162-166. https://
journals.sagepub.com/doi/full/10.1177/1745691617707315.

Brown, B. *Atlas of the Heart.* Random House, NY, NY 2021.

Jaquad, S., The Isolation Journal: https://theisolationjournals.
substack.com/.

Collins, S.K.. *Stillpoint: The Dance of Selfcaring, Selfhealing*, TLC Productions, 1992.

Wolfelt, A.D., Center for Loss and Life Transition, https://www.centerforloss.com/.

Grunes, M and Allardi, S *Feeling Stressed?* Read a poem, Nautilus, June 27, 2022, Feeling Stressed? Read a Poem - Nautilus.

Bates, J. and Byrne, P., *Stressed, Unstressed: Classic Poems to Ease the Mind.* William Collins, NY, NY 2017.

Frost, R. *Stopping by Woods on a Snowy Evening.* From the Poetry of Robert Frost, edited by Edward Connery, Harry Holt and Company, NY,NY 1923.

Langstroth, G., https://www.wordmoves.com/full.

Whyte, D., *Well of Grief,* https://allpoetry.com/poem/15379848-The-well-of-grief-by-David-Whyte.

Cohen, L., video of song Anthem: https://www.youtube.com/watch?v=1jzloNlTmzY.

Kierkegaard, S. Kierkegaard's Journals and Notebooks, ed. Niels-Jørgen Cappelørn et al. (Princeton, NJ: Princeton University Press, 2007.

Rom, Gabriel, Pingu, New York Times, Oct 16, 2022 https://nytimes.pressreader.com/article/281741273325197.

Playback Theater: https://playbacknorthamerica.com/about/.

10: Dance: Embodying Grief and Its Transformation

The Sun Dance is a Native American Ceremony, originally Lakota, done as a prayer for life. Seeking spiritual power, dancers take no food or water during the 4-days. The dance helps dancers to reconnect with the earth. https://study.com/academy/lesson/sun-dance-ceremony-practices-overview.html.

Dances of Universal Peace is a spiritual practice that employs singing and
dancing the sacred phrases of the world's religions. The intention
is to raise consciousness and promote peace.
https://www.dancesofuniversalpeace.org/.

Holmes, B. *Joy Unspeakable, Contemplative Practices of the Black Church*,
Fortress Press, Second Edition, Minneapolis, MN 2017.

Walker, A. *Calling All Grandmothers. In Hard Times Require Furious
Dancing*, New World Library, Novato, CA. 2010.

Research, Dance and the Healthy Brain P. 167-168):

Joe V.et. al, Leisure Activities and the Risk of Dementia in the Elderly,
The New England Journal of Medicine, June 19, 2003. https://www.
nejm.org/doi/pdf/10.1056/NEJMoa022252

Merom, D, et.al Cognitive Benefits of Social Dancing and Walking in Old
Age: The Dancing Mind Randomized Controlled Trial,
Neurocognitive Aging and Behavior, Feb 22 , 2016. Cognitive
Benefits of Social Dancing and Walking in Old Age: The Dancing
Mind Randomized Controlled Trial - PubMed (nih.gov)

Chunxiao W. et. al, Effects of Mind-Body Exercises on Cognitive Function
in Older Adults: A Meta-Analysis. *American Journal of Geriatrics*,
2019, April; 67(4):749-758. Effects of Mind-Body Exercises on
Cognitive Function in Older Adults: A Meta-Analysis - PubMed
(nih.gov)

Yosuke O., Exercise type of activities of daily living disability in older
women: An 8-year population-based cohort study, *Scandinavian
Journal of Medical Science Sports* 2019 Mar 29 (3):400-406
Exercise type and activities of daily living disability in
older women: An 8-year population-based cohort study -
PubMed (nih.gov)

Burzynska, A., et al., White Matter Integrity Declined Over 6-Months, but
Dance Intervention Improved Integrity of the Fornix of Older
Adults, *Front Aging Neuroscience* 2017 Mar 16:9:59 https://pubmed.
ncbi.nlm.nih.gov/28360853/

Unleashing the potential of dance: a neuroplasticity-based approach
bridging from older adults to Parkinson's disease patients,
Aging Neuroscience June 26, 2023, vol 15 https://www.frontiersin.
org/articles/10.3389/fnagi.2023.1188855/full.

Whitelaw, G. Wetzig, B., *Move to Greatness: Focusing the Four Essential
Energies of a Whole and Balanced Leader,* Nicholas Brealey
International, Boston, 2008, https://bit.ly/3FIGGme.

Armstrong, W., *Unspoken*, New Yorker Documentary, choreographer Paul
Lightfoot communicates one of the many goodbyes disrupted by
the coronavirus pandemic. https://www.newyorker.com/culture/the-
new-yorker-documentary/dancing-a-story-of-love-and-grief. 2022.

Dance Therapy In 1966, Marian Chace and other dancers founded the
American Dance Therapy Association: https://www.adta.org/

11: Music and Voice: Resonating and Resolving Grief

Sacks, O. *Musicophia: Tales of Music and the Brain.* Vintage, London, UK. 2008

M Stroebe, Schut H. The dual process model of coping with bereavement:
rationale and description, Death Study 1999 Apr-May; 23(3):197-224.

Malkin, G., is a seven-time Emmy award-winning composer and producer.
He creates music-driven media and experiences that inspire the
heart and catalyze individual and societal healing.
https://www.realmusic.com/artists/gary-remal-malkin/

Mead, M. https://awcpittsburgh.com/sound-healing/

Malkin, M. *Graceful Passages: A Companion for Living and Dying,* Book and
album, https://garymalkin.bandcamp.com/album/graceful-
passages-a-companion-for-living-and-dying

Collins, S.K., *Warrior Mother: Fierce Love, Unbearable Loss and Rituals that
Heal,* She Writes Press, 2013.

Sacks, Oliver, *Musicophia: Tales of Music and the Brain,* New York, Vintage Books, 2008

Malkin, Gary, Stillwater, Michael, *Graceful Passages,* Album, Wisdom of the World Wellness:

Music for a Meaningful Life, https://www.wisdomoftheworld.com/

Rachmaninoff, S., Rhapsody on a Theme of Paganini, https://www.youtube.com/watch?v=ppJ5uITLECE

Engaging with Music 2022 Report, *International Federation of the Phonographic Industry,* a global report on how people around the world enjoy an engage with music, 44,000 people in 22 countries. https://www.ifpi.org/ifpi-releases-engaging-with-music-2022-report/

Stevens, B., *Don't Push the River, It Flows by Itself,* The Gestalt Journal Press, Gouldsboro, ME 2005

Johann Sebastian Bach's Brandenburg Concerto No. 1 is the first work in a set of six of the best-known instrumental works from the first half of the 18th century. https://www.youtube.com/watch?v=BOZEj8wyj-I

Larson, J. *Season's of Love.* Album; Rent (Original Broadway Cast Recording.) Dreamworks. 1996.

Threshold Choir. https://thresholdchoir.org/

Wolfgang A.M. *Requiem,* https://www.youtube.com/watch?v=G7KNmW9a75Y

Music Therapy is an allied healthcare profession that offers music interventions in healthcare settings: https://www.musictherapy.org/about/musictherapy/.

Dubois, W.E.B., *The Souls of Black Folk.* Project Gutenberg, 2011. https://www.gutenberg.org/files/408/408-h/408-h.htm.

Sorrow songs – songs that expressed the suffering and unjust treatment of enslaved African Americans: https:// pages.stolaf.edu/americanmusic/2022/10/11/african-american-sorrow-songs-and- spirituals/

12: Visual Arts and Architecture:
Memorializing Memories

German, V., at The Frick Pittsburgh Reckoning: Grief and Light – Part 2 of
2 https://www.youtube.com/watch?v=Zc6lXrpul9M

Miller, M. Mary Miller Dance Company. https://www.linkedin.com/in/mary-
miller-1a10633b/

Wingless, J, and Fields-Black, E. *"Unburied, Unmourned, Unmarked:
Requiem for Rice."* Carnegie Music Hall., 2019. https://www.
thefrickpittsburgh.org/uuu

Baker, M., https://www.mbodiedart.studio/about-michelle-baker

Taylor, G., One and All Wisdom: https://oneandallwisdom.com/

Winton-Henry, C. multimedia artist: https://www.facebook.com/
ShrineWorkshop/

Vietnam Memorial: https://www.youtube.com/watch?v=fVCXF6PNog4&t=140s

Furstenberg, S.B. art installation 2021, In America Remember
https://www.suzannefirstenberg.com/in-america-remember

National Memorial for Peace and Justice: https://legacysites.eji.org/

Yeh, L., TEDx Cornell University https://www.youtube.com/
watch?v=fVCXF6PNog4&t=140s

The Barefoot Artist, 2014 film: https://barefootartists.org/the-barefoot-
artist-documentary/

The National 9/11 Memorial: https://www.911memorial.org/

Flight 93 Memorial National Memorial Pennsylvania: https://www.nps.gov/
flni/index.htm

RED Dress Project National Museum of the American Indian Washington
DC: https://americanindian.si.edu/explore/exhibitions/item?id=973

Davidson, Justin, *Sandy Hook Memorial - Out of Horror, Beauty, A Visit to the New Sandy Hook Memorial,* Architecture Review: The Sandy Hook Memorial (curbed.com). 2022.

Michele Baker: https://www.mbodiedart.studio/home

Art Therapy a mental health profession that works with individuals, families, and communities using artmaking within a psychotherapeutic relationship: https://arttherapy.org/

13: Curating Our Experiences Towards an Artful Life

Collins, S.K. *The Pearl.* Unpublished poem, 2011.

LaBalme, V. *Risk Forward: Embrace the Unknown and Unlock Your Hidden Genius,* Hay House Inc. Carlsbad, CA 2021

10/27 Healing Partnership – This Pittsburgh non-profit provides support, connection, and opportunities for reflection for individuals and their loved ones impacted by the October 2018 Tree of Life Synagogue Shooting and for others who experience hate-induced trauma. Many programs and events are open to the whole community. https://1027healingpartnership.org/history/

Violins of Hope is a project of concerts based on a private collection of holocaust-related violins,Violas and cellos have been collected since the end of World War II. "All instruments have a common denominator: they are symbols of hope and a way to say: remember me, remember us. Life is good; celebrate it for those who perished and for those who survived. For all people." https://www.violins-of-hope.com/

Chicago, J. Jewish Women's Archive. ""Merger Poem Poster" by Judy Chicago, 1988." (Viewed on February 6, 2024) https://jwa.org/media/chicago-judy-1-still-image.

Index

A

B

C

F

G

H

I

Acknowledgements

It takes a village to write a book and get it out into the larger world, which means it would take way too many pages to roll the credits on this art project and name everyone that contributed.

But I begin by honoring the memory of my two children, Kenneth Collins and Corinne Weber, whose illnesses and deaths set me on this journey of the connection between grief and the arts. Appreciations are due to the people who responded, (or not) to my previous book, Warrior Mother–you taught me the importance of embracing grieving, to not miss out on the fullness of life it can bring. To the students and staff at Bluffton University in Ohio, appreciation for showing me how hungry young people are for art tools to overcome losses in their lives. I offer a special thanks to the people who attended my first Art of Grieving keynote at a Pittsburgh synagogue in 2017, and to media consultant Lydia Blank who came up with the title and got me booked.

To my collaborators and playmates, members of The Wing & a Prayer Pittsburgh Players–Pam Meadowcroft, Lynn Coghill, Laverne Baker Hotep, Lois McClendon, Richard Citrin, Shari Mastalski, (and her artist mother Gloria), Gail Ransom, Laurie Tartar, Bob Wilson, Brandi Lee, and Elizabeth Downing–recognition for the nearly two decades of our performing together, stories of our experiences of love and loss, including poignant moments like supporting troupe member Jim Holland in his final days. My creative journey has been enriched by enduring partnerships–with co-author/

collaborator Christine Gautreaux, mentor/teacher Cynthia Winton-Henry, and life partner, husband Richard Citrin. This book, like me, is because they are.

I extend much gratitude to readers of my weekly blog, many of whom engaged in email conversations about it, helping me clarify my thinking to become a better writer. Special acknowledgment goes to the Sisters of Divine Providence and the Sisters of St Joseph at Baden, for the opportunity to explore the art of grieving in their centuries' old communities, highlighting the important role of art in ritual and the critical role of ritual in transforming grief. Much appreciation to members of the international InterPlay community who met with me on-line when in-person events shut down, and to the online platform Let's Reimagine for providing a space to collaborate with artists Trish Watts, Cynthia Winton Henry, Soyinka Rahim, Mairi Campbell, Wai-Chin Matsuoka, and the larger Reimagine community and their rituals of remembrance. Thanks to colleagues, friends, and coaching clients for sharing the art forms they practice and for allowing me to use snippets of their stories to illustrate how the arts transform grief. In the book's production phase much credit goes to artist, editor, and book coach Amanda Filippelli, who was already practicing the art of grieving when I met her in the spring of 2023 at her interactive art installation, The Remembering Room, a work she created in response to the sudden death of her father. Cover and book designer Christa Varley used her unique skill set to capture the essence of my body of written work, in the colors and designs for this present one.

Before ending I must deeply honor those, who due to our close family ties, taught me the most about the challenges and gifts of grieving, granddaughter Kyra Joy, her mother Jody Curtis, her father, Kevin Collins, and my husband Rich Citrin.

I must not forget family members who left their earthly lives during the writing of this book; siblings Patricia Gusman, Mary Jane Smith, Maureen Ackley, and former husband George Collins. Each exit deepened my understanding and appreciation for what a gift to my life their lives have been and will continue to be.

As I begin my happy dance of releasing this book into the larger world, I picture balloons, streamers, and a marching band to help me express my unending gratitude to those who will take it out into the world and ensure that it delivers its gifts to those in need of them.

Sheila K. Collins

Sheila K Collins, PhD knows grief, having lost a son to AIDS and a daughter to breast cancer, experiences she chronicled in her award-winning memoir, Warrior Mother: Fierce Love, Unbearable Loss and the Rituals that Heal, published by She Writes Press in 2013. Her 40-year career as a therapist, professor of social worker, and author has followed her experience as a professional dancer. Applying wisdom gleaned from that career, she has guided thousands of people through the tough challenges life handed them—inspiring them to turn grief into a gift. She's delighted audiences worldwide with demonstrations of how art-based expressions, such as dance, storytelling, song, and music, can help anyone turn life's toughest challenges into growth. Her 2016 TEDx talk, When Death Threatens Someone We Love, offers a poignant perspective for anyone accompanying a loved one through life-threatening illness and death. Her first book, released in 2018 for a second edition and co-authored with Christine Gautreaux, Stillpoint: A Self-Care Playbook for Caregivers to Find Ease and Time to Breathe and Reclaim Joy has become a popular online course for professional and family caregivers.

Sheila currently directs the Wing & A Prayer Pittsburgh Players, an InterPlay-based performance troupe that helps individuals and organizations tell their stories in transforming ways. Sheila and her partner of 45 years, international consultant, and leadership coach Richard Citrin, live in Pittsburgh Pennsylvania. For keynote speaking and consultations reach Sheila through her website https://sheilakcollins.com/

If you have enjoyed this book and found it helpful and believe it would be helpful to others, please take a few moments to review it on Amazon.